A WORD AND A SONG

A 52-WEEK CHRISTIAN DEVOTIONAL OF SCRIPTURE AND HYMNS

NORMAN JONES

Edited by
BETTY JONES

Published © 2021. Norman Jones.
Editor and Contributions by Betty Jones
Editor, Contributions, and Publishing Assistance
by Angela Jones
Cover copyright © 2021 Norman Jones
Cover Design by Angela Jones

This book is a work of non-fiction. The opinions expressed represent and belong to the author alone. Material not created by the author is accordingly credited to the correlating authors or owners and those rights are retained by those persons or entities. The author of this work by no means or in any terms claims any credit or rights for any text otherwise quoted or cited in this book. Please refer to the Reference List for more information on works exempt from the author's claim.

Tri-Blood Publishing
www.tribloodpublishing.com

CONTENTS

Introduction ix

1. WEEK ONE 1
   Leisure 2
   I Need Thee Every Hour 4

2. WEEK TWO 6
   When We Walk With the Lord 8

3. WEEK THREE 10
   Why Does God Not Answer? 11
   My Faith Looks Up to Thee 13

4. WEEK FOUR 14
   I Hear Thy Welcome Voice / Gwahoddiad 16

5. WEEK FIVE 19
   Fight the Good Fight 21

6. WEEK SIX 23
   Easter 25

7. WEEK SEVEN 27
   Man of Sorrows 29

8. WEEK EIGHT 31
   Leaning on the Everlasting Arms 33

9. WEEK NINE 35
   Standing on the Promises 37

10. WEEK TEN 40
    Blessed Assurance 42

11.	WEEK ELEVEN	44
	Love Divine, All Loves Excelling	46
12.	WEEK TWELVE	48
	Master, Speak! Thy Servant Heareth	50
13.	WEEK THIRTEEN	52
	Sweet Hour of Prayer	54
14.	WEEK FOURTEEN	56
	Mighty God, While Angels Bless Thee	58
15.	WEEK FIFTEEN	60
	Serenity Prayer	61
	He Keeps Me Singing	62
16.	WEEK SIXTEEN	64
	'Tis so Sweet to Trust in Jesus	66
17.	WEEK SEVENTEEN	68
	The Chemistry of Character	69
	I Heard the Voice of Jesus Say	70
	Love Lifted Me	72
18.	WEEK EIGHTEEN	74
	O Mighty God	77
19.	WEEK NINETEEN	79
	O God, Our Help in Ages Past	81
20.	WEEK TWENTY	83
	Joyful, Joyful, We Adore Thee	85
21.	WEEK TWENTY-ONE	88
	Sing to the Lord a Joyful Song	90
22.	WEEK TWENTY-TWO	92
	All the Way My Savior Leads Me	94

23. WEEK TWENTY-THREE	97
Enough to Know	99
24. WEEK TWENTY-FOUR	101
Come, Thou Fount of Every Blessing	103
25. WEEK TWENTY-FIVE	106
He Sent His Word and Healed Them	108
26. WEEK TWENTY-SIX	110
America (My Country 'Tis of Thee)	113
27. WEEK TWENTY-SEVEN	115
Immortal, Invisible	118
28. WEEK TWENTY-EIGHT	120
Jesus Calls Us O'er the Tumult	121
Come Thou Almighty King	123
29. WEEK TWENTY-NINE	126
Through the Year	127
All Things Bright and Beautiful	128
30. WEEK THIRTY	130
Abide with Me	132
31. WEEK THIRTY-ONE	134
God Will Take Care of You	136
32. WEEK THIRTY-TWO	138
A Mighty Fortress Is Our God	140
33. WEEK THIRTY-THREE	143
Jesus Lives, and So Shall I	145
34. WEEK THIRTY-FOUR	147
O Love That Will Not Let Me Go	149

35. WEEK THIRTY-FIVE	151
God's Garden	152
In The Garden	154
36. WEEK THIRTY-SIX	156
When Morning Gilds the Skies	158
37. WEEK THIRTY-SEVEN	160
For the Beauty of the Earth	162
38. WEEK THIRTY-EIGHT	164
Ode to Face Masks	166
Thanks be to God	167
39. WEEK THIRTY-NINE	169
O Come, O Come, Emmanuel	171
40. WEEK FORTY	173
Blest Be the Tie that Binds	175
Hail, Thou Long Expected Jesus	176
41. WEEK FORTY-ONE	178
O Little Town of Bethlehem	180
42. WEEK FORTY-TWO	183
Good King Wenceslas	185
43. WEEK FORTY-THREE	188
We Three Kings	191
44. WEEK FORTY-FOUR	193
Psalm 24	194
Jesus, the Very Thought of Thee	196
45. WEEK FORTY-FIVE	198
Wonderful Peace	201
46. WEEK FORTY-SIX	202
Just a Closer Walk with Thee	204

47. WEEK FORTY-SEVEN	206
Isle of Beauty	207
My Jesus, I Love Thee	209
48. WEEK FORTY-EIGHT	211
Great is Thy Faithfulness	214
49. WEEK FORTY-NINE	216
Praise to the Lord, the Almighty	218
50. WEEK FIFTY	221
I Walk with the King	223
Watchman Tell Us of the Night	224
51. WEEK FIFTY-ONE	226
Glorious Things of Thee are Spoken	228
52. WEEK FIFTY-TWO	231
We've a Story to Tell to the Nations	233
Afterword	235
Reference List	237
About the Author	247
Listen & Sing Along!	249

INTRODUCTION

The beauty of a Christian life is that you never know when yet another opportunity will come your way. And that is exactly what happened nearly six years ago when I was asked to lead a new Bible study group organized in the Tara Woods Community. It was to be an outreach activity from our nearby Holy Trinity Presbyterian Church and they needed a leader!

I volunteered and, within a very short space of time, 10:00am on Tuesday mornings became a life changing event. The Estate gave us the use of a delightfully furnished room within their Activities building and we had a home.

Every Tuesday morning from then on became a couple of hours of pure pleasure as we studied the Scriptures with prayer and music – always music. I used the word 'pleasure' for that is what it became to all. Pleasure in His word, pleasure in the reading, pleasure in the music, and pleasure and friendship as only Christian sisters and brothers can enjoy.

Then came the COVID-19! And, as in the entire country, all such activities were banned and America went into lockdown.

But! Tuesday mornings were still going to keep coming around and what about the Word and the Music? Simply, we had to resort to the printed form of communication and that began on March 8th, 2020.

The first letter to the Tara Woods Bible Study Group included a hymn which turned out to be an important part of the weekly message encouraging the Group that, above all else, it was necessary that we continue our studies AND that we sing!

The words to the weekly hymn were included along with a story about the author and an invitation to sing whether you were washing dishes, preparing dinner, or whatever. When we sing, we keep the Spirit active within us – so sing!

From then on, it became my pleasure to write a weekly letter to all of our members with simply a word and a song. Hence the name of this book! I sincerely hope this weekly devotional helps lift your spirit and draw you closer to the Lord no matter what life may be throwing your way.

Sincerely,

Norman Jones

WEEK ONE

March 10, 2020

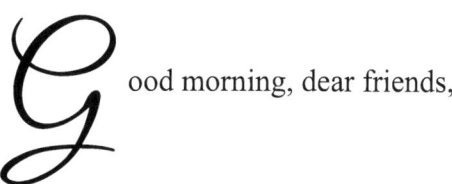ood morning, dear friends,

Well here we go, the first week after 'lockdown', as we experience a very different 'Tuesday morning'. Fortunately, being in the 'computer age', we at least have some communication through this email. The joy of our weekly meeting can still be possible though prayer and song. One of the highlights of our meetings was the closing song – and that can go on as you will see as you read. The opening statement JAMES 5:16 is so perfectly right for the times we are in and we are able to follow his guidance no matter where we may be. What a beautiful sentence of Scripture, "Therefore confess your sins to each other and pray for each other so that you may be healed. The prayer of a righteous person is powerful and effective."

The Rev. John Brown must have experienced some difficulty three hundred years ago when he wrote, "There is great need of patience in this world, where wickedness and distress abound. But it is very honorable to accommodate our religion in our lives. To give ourselves to effective, fervent prayer for ourselves and others, to be always ready to humbly acknowledge our faults."

One of my favorite poems from my school days was by William Henry Davies. With the advent of the motor car in the early 1900s, he was moved to write his feelings on the changing world when he wrote this poem and titled it simply "Leisure".

LEISURE

What is this world if full of care,
We have no time to stand and stare.

*No time to stand beneath the boughs
And stare as long as sheep or cows.*

*No time to see when woods we pass,
Where squirrels hide their nuts in grass.*

*No time to see in broad daylight,
Streams full of stars like skies at night.*

*A poor life this if full of care,
We have no time to stand and stare.*

Heavenly Father, please strengthen our hearts and remind us to encourage one another when the troubles of life start to overwhelm us. Please guard our hearts from depression. Give us the strength to rise up each day and fight through prayer against the struggles which weigh us down. Amen.

From the poetry of Willian Davies to the very special words of Annie Sherwood Hawks who wrote many hymns for Sunday School books. Annie shows her feelings in the hymn "I Need Thee Every Hour". Enjoy.

I NEED THEE EVERY HOUR

(Verse 1)
I need Thee every hour,
Most gracious Lord;
No tender voice like Thine
Can peace afford.

(Chorus)
I need Thee, O I need Thee;
Every hour I need Thee!
O bless me now my Saviour,
I come to Thee.

(Verse 2)
I need Thee every hour,
Stay Thou nearby,
Temptations lose their power
When Thou art nigh.

(Verse 3)
I need Thee every hour,
In joy or pain;
Come quickly and abide,
Or life is vain.

(Verse 4)
I need Thee every hour,
Most Holy One;
O make me Thine indeed,
Thou blessed Son.

What a wonderful reminder of our need for Him who always provides when we ask. Keep us constantly in Your care dear Lord.

Rich blessings and love to all,
Betty & Norman

WEEK TWO

March 17, 2020

ood morning, dear friends,

The time is 6:30 a.m. and I have just watched four episodes of Andy Griffith and Mayberry – oh what a simpler time in life! Now I am ready to begin another day of isolation. Well, not total isolation. I have my Betty who keeps baking some of my favorite cakes and pastries – look out waistline!

However, I have spent a good deal of time in thought

– without watching the news – and several words entered my mind that caused me to pay attention. In times of crises, we are faced with words that prove to add more meaning to the times we are living in and I chose three: Fear…Patience…Trust.

Fear is to have an uneasy anticipation, causing us to be afraid – and that is not unusual in this troubled time. However, we have the encouraging words of PSALM 91 which is full of the assurances of God's protection. This Psalm is so complete with words like shelter, refuge, shield, deliver, presence, rescue. This wonderful reading speaks of God's power, presence, and protection against fear. These telling words are meant to cover and comfort us with security in these difficult times.

Patience is a virtue – so they tell us – and this word is common throughout the Bible. 1 SAMUEL reads, "Lack of patience can cause us to miss blessings". Being patient is a vital part of trusting in God, particularly as we go through these difficult and trying times.

Trust, what a wonderful word! It means: a firm belief, strength, confident expectation, reliance on the truth, bold and sure security. Trusting is what we do because of the faith we have been given. Trusting is believing in the promises of God in all circumstances. And it is by this trust in Him, that we are promised peace. AMEN.

With all that said, we can now turn our thoughts to a Brooklyn born songwriter. John Sammis. After moving to Indiana at age twenty-two, he was converted to Christianity and spent many years with the YMCA before becoming a Presbyterian minister. He also, during his busy life, found time to write more than one hundred hymns and in line with the times I have chosen his wonderful message, "Trust and Obey", also known as "When We Walk with the Lord".

WHEN WE WALK WITH THE LORD

>(Verse 1)
>*When we walk with the Lord*
>*In the light of His word,*
>*What a glory He sheds on our way.*
>*While we do His goodwill,*
>*He abides with us still,*
>*And with all who will trust and obey.*
>
>(Chorus)
>*Trust and obey,*
>*For there's no other way*
>*To be happy in Jesus,*

But to trust and obey.

(Verse 3)
But we never can prove
The delights of His love,
Until all on the altar we lay;
For the favor He shows
And the joy He bestows.
Are for them who will trust and obey.

Rich blessings to all as you walk with the Lord in the light of His word.
    Betty & Norman

WEEK THREE

March 24, 2020

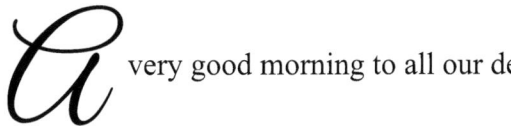 very good morning to all our dear friends,

I find it interesting that as the virus goes on, how much more frequent I see messages on the computer reminding people the need for prayer. In fact, a few such messages from people that are accustomed to using the Lord's name in vain. This made me wonder what they are expecting from our dear Lord – and more important, will they recognize when He answers. Reflecting on this is the following poem by my granddaughter, who writes under the name Talis Jones, that I would like to share:

WHY DOES GOD NOT ANSWER?

>"God," they whisper, hushed and quiet.
>"Speak to me, O please."
>Wind danced through the leaves
>Birds sang from the branches
>"No answer," they sigh in the breeze.
>
>"God," they say louder, needing to be heard.
>"Appear to me, O please."
>A deer glides through the woods
>A rainbow beams in the dew
>"No answer," they glare at the trees.
>
>"God", they shout, impatient now.
>"Touch me, O please."
>Gently a butterfly kisses their shoulder
>A brief gale caresses their cheek
>"No answer," they spit in unease.

"God", they cry, despair seizing their
    throats.
"Please help me, O please."
A neighbor knocks at the door
The church bell rings by the shore
"No answer," they fall to their knees.

"Child," God whispers, undeterred.
"Hear me, O please.
Open your heart, take my hand.
Let me help you, please stand.
"No answer," God sighs with the seas.

What a beautiful reminder that God is always around us in many ways including the little simple things we take for granted.

Our Hymnist this week is Ray Palmer who went from school to be a grocer's assistant but at an early age underwent a religious awakening. He studied for the ministry and was ordained in 1835 in the Congregational Union. He proved to be a popular preacher and in addition excelled in writing poetry and hymns. Today we sing one of his most popular hymns, "My Faith Looks Up to Thee".

A WORD AND A SONG

MY FAITH LOOKS UP TO THEE

(Verse 1)
My faith looks up to Thee,
Thou Lamb of Calvary,
Savior divine.
Now hear me while pray,
Take all my guilt away
O let me from this day
Be wholly Thine!

(Verse 2)
May Thy rich grace impart
Strength to my fainting heart,
My zeal inspire.
As Thou hast died for me,
O may my love to Thee,
Pure warm and changeless
Be a living fire.

Blessings dear friends, be safe and well.
    Betty & Norman

WEEK FOUR

March 31, 2020

ood morning friends, one and all!

Well, that has been another *long* week! I remember when my favorite saying was "Time goes by too fast!" I do trust and pray that these notes find you and yours are both safe and well.

Once again, we have the book of James to thank for the words we studied many weeks ago. I spent these last few days reading back to lesson No. 1, "Growing

Through Trials". Right from the start we read words that are so supportive in these difficult days. JAMES 1:2-3 "My brethren, and what a word 'patience' has become, count it all joy when you fall into various trials, knowing that the testing of your faith produces patience." What wonderful words to give us courage to see this present problem through. My dictionary describes patience as "calm endurance" or "Perseverance". I see in my study notes I wrote "Ask God for wisdom and have no doubts about the outcome."

The virus almost stopped the release of the new movie "I Still Believe", but it is now on DVD, Blu-ray, and Digital Home Video. It tells the story of Christian singer Jeremy Camp, whose first wife died of ovarian cancer. Shortly after, Camp wrote the song "I Still Believe". The film producer said, "Life's full of things that we can't control and things that don't go according to plan. The whole thing about the movie is "I Still Believe" – even when I can't see."

I am sure that you all join Betty and I in praying for the day when we can begin to return to 'normal' and we know that that day will come soon. A favorite song of ours that I think may help lift your spirits is "I Believe in Miracles". This song, by Carlton Buck and John Peterson, was used as the theme song for Kathryn Kuhlman's show in the 60's and 70's. She was said to be one of the greatest women preachers of her day. You may remember this tune and perhaps even have it already playing in your thoughts, but if not then I encourage you to give this rousing hymn a listen.

Together today let us sing a beautiful hymn you may or may not be familiar with. Originally written by an American minister, Lewis Hartsough, in 1872 it was shortly after translated into Welsh by minister Ieuan Gwyllt and has since become a popular hymn sung in Wales, so much so that many believe the song of Welsh origin! I have Welsh in my own heritage and discovering hymns written in both English and Welsh is a special find to my heart. I most certainly hope you will take a moment to listen to this hymn in both languages.

I HEAR THY WELCOME VOICE / GWAHODDIAD

> (Verse 1)
> *I hear Thy welcome voice*
> *That calls me, Lord, to Thee,*
> *For cleansing in Thy precious blood*
> *That flowed on Calvary.*

(Chorus)
I am coming, Lord!
Coming now to Thee!
Wash me, cleanse me in the blood
That flowed on Calvary!

(Verse 1 – Welsh)
Mi gylwaf dyner lais
Yn galw arnaf fi
I ddod a golchi 'meiau gyd
Yn afon Calfari

(Chorus – Welsh)
Arglwydd dyma fi
Ar dy alwad di
Golch fi'n burlan yn y gwaed
A gaed ar galfari

(Verse 2)
Tho' coming weak and vile,
Thou dost my strength assure;
Thou dost my vileness fully cleanse,
Till spotless all, and pure.

(Chorus)
I am coming, Lord!

Coming now to Thee!
Wash me, cleanse me in the blood
That flowed on Calvary!

Arglwydd dyma fi
Ar dy alwad di
Golch fi'n burlan yn y gwaed
A gaed ar galfari

The merciful invitation and love of God is a miracle indeed! Amen!

We wish everyone a prayer filled week!
    In our Saviour's love,
    Betty & Norman

WEEK FIVE

April 7, 2020

ood morning, dear friends, in His name,

I noticed this week on Facebook a discussion about what is going to happen to the lovely old, but abandoned, Methodist church in my hometown. There were several suggestions ranging from demolition, to carpet shop, to dance hall, but no one mentioned the service it had provided for many years as the village church. Then someone questioned the need for the building in the first place. That started me thinking what such a person would think if you mentioned the Bible in the old church. That led me to think how I might answer such a question as "Why the Bible?"

With help from the BOOK OF JAMES, here are some answers:

WHY THE BIBLE?
The Bible is Divinely inspired.
The Bible is proven in science.
The Bible is food for the soul.
The Bible is education.
The Bible is wisdom.
The Bible develops insight and demands study.
The Bible is all of these things
BUT MOST OF ALL, **IT IS LOVE**.

That is why we study the Bible. Not because we expect you to major in theology, but so that you will show that you are a listener and a doer of the Word. So that you will reap the rewards of perseverance. So that you can learn to grow through trials. So that you will have more love, more compassion, more gentleness, and more goodness. So that you will be closer to a God bigger than the world.

In short, you can enjoy more life through knowing and understanding the greatness of God through His son, Jesus Christ.

Such treatment of a fine old House of God really demands some answers and I think perhaps the words of our hymn this week by John Monsell provide an answer. Rector Monsell was a well-educated minister and also known as a strong advocate for our Lord. He was an Irishman and served several churches in Ireland before being transferred to England. Sadly, at the last church he served in England he was killed in a construction accident. Before his end, he wrote the great hymn "Fight the Good Fight".

FIGHT THE GOOD FIGHT

> *Fight the good fight with all thy might,*
> *Christ is thy strength and all thy might.*
> *Lay hold on Life, and it shall be.*
> *Thy joy and crown eternally.*

> *Run thou the race of God's good grace,*

Lift up thine eyes and seek His face.
Life with it's way before us lies,
Christ is the path and Christ the prize.

Cast care aside, lean on thy guide,
Thy every need He will provide;
Trusting in Him will ever prove,
Christ is thy life, thy hope, thy love

Faint not nor fear, His arms are near,
He changeth not and thou art dear.
Only believe, and thou shalt see
That Christ is all in all to thee.

Amen.

Dear friends, your every need He will provide.
    Betty & Norman

WEEK SIX

April 14, 2020

*H*E IS RISEN! HE IS RISEN INDEED.

There can be no better way to open a letter than these seven words. Amen. I trust you will not mind a slight departure from the usual tone in this week's letter. The reason is, I had a couple of experiences this past week that are worth mention and frankly, just want to share them with you.

Many years ago, I hired a young salesman named Greg and was immediately struck by his attitude to life.

He proved to be a young man of living faith, and showed it from the start. He also proved to be a very good salesman and a genuine friend. Our ways parted for many years until I had the good fortune to see his name on Facebook on my computer. He had married and they had two daughters and were living in West Palm Beach. I contacted him and very sadly discovered that he was now suffering from Lou Gehrig's disease. But what struck me most was that he still had that beautiful positive attitude of years gone by and so easily talked of his deep faith in God and his future.

Last week, during my prayers, Greg's name up, and as I prayed, a hymn came to mind so I just had to write him the words to "Great is Thy faithfulness, O God my Father". His response was to tell me that in a quiet moment that week, he had had the tune going through his mind but didn't know all the words. I was so glad to have furnished them, Amen.

Next, we are reminded that Easter, according to modern day practices of many, is about eggs, rabbits, and assorted gifts etc. But we Christians know it is much more in our lives than that. I asked permission to use some very special words written by a member of our Bible group, Ann Scott, and here they are:

EASTER

> *Easter is not about bunnies, or bright*
> *   colored eggs it is true.*
> *Easter is more than The Old Rugged*
> *   Cross, Easter is all about you.*
>
> *Easter is not about music, or pageants and*
> *   dramas to view.*
> *Easter is more about the empty tomb,*
> *   Easter is all about you.*
>
> *Easter is how you view Jesus, and what*
> *   your heart tells you to do.*
> *He shed His life's blood to save you.*
> *   Easter is all about you.*
>
> *Easter is blood bought redemption; God's*
> *   gift for each Gentile and Jew.*
> *Easter's about your salvation. Easter is all*
> *   about you.*
>
> *Easter proclaims resurrection: Without*
> *   which our faith would undo.*
> *But because He lives, you can live also.*
> *   Easter is all about you.*

*So what will you do now with Jesus? Your
just —-being neutral—won't do.
He has done all He can do to save you.
Now, Easter is all about you.*

∼

Thank you, Ann. So beautifully written with Easter and us in mind.

I also encourage you to listen to the words of Gloria and Bill Gaither's beautiful hymn "Because He lives" (1971) as it captures the deep hope and truth for us all thanks to the great sacrifice Jesus Christ made on our behalf.

And that, our dear friends, says it all for now. Have a blessed week as you live in His name.

Much Christian love to all,

Betty & Norman

WEEK SEVEN

⊗

April 21, 2020

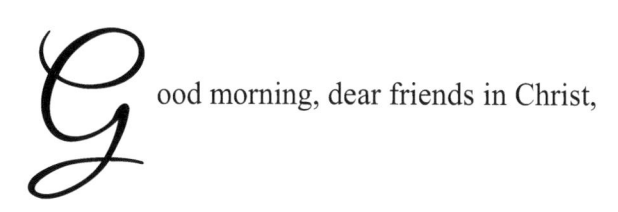

*G*ood morning, dear friends in Christ,

Even now, a week later, it still seems strange that we were not in church to celebrate the wonders of Easter and all it means to us Christians. Thanks to modern wonders, we at least had an 'electronic' connection to our churches.

Of course, there are always two sides to a story – or so they say. And I think that the other side to our story this year is that we certainly had more time to think of

Easter, and it gave us more time to celebrate the victory of Jesus over both sin and death followed by His glorious resurrection from the grave – the very basis for our faith. It is well for us to remember the words from 2 Timothy 2:11 – "It is a faithful saying: for if we be dead with Him, we shall also live with Him." To which the choir sings, "HALLELUJAH!"

I really enjoy the 'positives' that happen in times like these (sounds like a cue for a song). The London Royal Choral Society has performed the Hallelujah Chorus for 144 years, only missing twice when Hitler dropped bombs on London. This year, thanks again for technology, all 82 members of the choir recorded themselves singing at home. The videos were then somehow 'stitched' together. The result being the production appeared as usual on Good Friday. How very wonderful.

At least, we now have time to study and prepare for our next course on Proverbs as we travel back some 3,000 years to spend time with King Solomon. I have seen the Book of Proverbs described as a 'collection of collections', also as an anthology (A collection of choice selections from literature) – even a 'scrapbook'. So, we are in for some interesting times at Tara Woods. Keep on praying for the day we can 'congregate' again.

I mentioned a cue for a song and here is one written for the occasion by Philip Bliss called "Man of Sorrows".

Sing it fast or slow, with triumph or reflection, whatever your soul is called to do. Hallelujah!

∼

MAN OF SORROWS

>(Verse 1)
>*Man of sorrows what a name*
>*For the Son of God, who came*
>*Ruined sinners to reclaim:*
>*Hallelujah, what a Savior!*
>
>(Verse 4)
>*He was lifted up to die;*
>*"It is finished" was His cry;*
>*Now in Heaven exalted high:*
>*Hallelujah, what a Savior!*
>
>(Verse 5)
>*When He comes, our glorious King,*
>*All His ransomed home to bring,*
>*Then anew this song we'll sing:*
>*Hallelujah, what a Savior!*

∼

Another song I think is quite appropriate for these strange and trying days is "In Times Like These" by Ruth Jones. Ruth and her husband Bert presented a weekly program on radio back in the 1940's called "A Visit with the Jones". Enjoy the well-chosen words as you go through the week.

Psalm 92:1 "It is a good thing to give thanks unto the Lord, and to sing praises unto Thy name, O most High."

Blessings and love to all in His precious name.
    Betty & Norman

WEEK EIGHT

April 28, 2020

Good morning to our dear friends in Christ,

We trust you are all safe and well.

We were fortunate enough to see Max Lucado for a brief two minutes on Fox News this week. He spoke of the loneliness and distress being experienced by many during these days. He went on to say that we were experiencing God's dynamic call from Heaven. He said our need for life, hope, and joy can be cured by our 'vertical' relationship with God. In addressing the difficulties of political separation, he said that we cannot love our neighbors till we learn to love and be loved by God.

An appropriate comment from my friend Rev. John Brown. 270 years ago, he wrote in his reflections on JOHN 20:31. "Great is the mercy that we have, directed by the Holy Spirit, to the eternal salvation of our souls. If we love Him much, through darkness and danger, we shall push our way into His presence."

This little saying appeared on Facebook this week and I liked it in its simplest terms: "THE HAPPINESS OF YOUR LIFE DEPENDS ON THE QUALITY OF YOUR THOUGHTS." It seems appropriate to me, as I have for many years used the term "Think good things" to folks experiencing difficult times.

Remember friends, you are never alone while God is saying, "Let me be your source of strength." Which leads me to a song by Anthony Showalter and Elisha Hoffman. Anthony was writing a letter of condolence to a former student and was inspired by a passage from DEUTERONOMY 33:27. And I can see why. If you don't know the melody just sit back, relax, and read "Leaning on the Everlasting Arms".

∼

LEANING ON THE EVERLASTING ARMS

(Verse 1)
What a fellowship, what a joy divine,
Leaning on the everlasting arms;
What a blessedness, what a peace is mine,
Leaning on the everlasting arms.

(Refrain)
Leaning, leaning, safe and secure from all alarms;
Leaning, leaning, leaning on the everlasting arms

(Verse 2)
O how sweet to walk, In this pilgrim way,
Leaning on the everlasting arms;
O how bright the path grows from day to day,
Leaning on the everlasting arms.

(Refrain)

(Verse 3)
What have I to dread, what have I to fear,
Leaning on the everlasting arms;

> *I have blessed peace with my Lord so near,*
> *Leaning on the everlasting arms.*

Rich blessings dear friends – and think good things!
   Betty & Norman

WEEK NINE

~~~

May 5, 2020

*G*ood morning to the Tuesday morning warriors,

Psalm 67:1 "God be merciful unto us, and bless us; and cause His face to smile on us."

Did you know that you can still smile when you are wearing a mask? It's true. Try it! The giveaway is your eyes. You smile with your eyes. Psalm 31:16 "Who can show us anything good? Smile upon us Lord." The fact that we continue to be 'locked down' doesn't give us much time to smile to anyone. But this week I went to Home Depot a couple of times for more 'stuff' for Betty's new garden. The staff there were wonderful – except for the checkout lady. PSALM 39:13 "Stop looking at me with chastisement, so I can smile again." So I tried a masked smile – and it worked!

Now you must be asking yourself what this has to do with my weekly note – everything my friends. We have never had a better chance to show our love for the Lord than the present days. There is a vast shortage of love going around at the present time and we can make someone's day with our Christian smile – and it works. I left the Home Depot with a now smiling check out lady and let me say that it made me feel better to see her smile. So we both benefitted from the experience. PSALM 80:3 "O God, restore us! Smile on us! Then we will be delivered."

We are so fortunate that because of our chosen life, our favorite book gives us so much to rely on. The word 'love' appears 310 times in the Bible and we are encouraged 365 times with the phrase "Do not be afraid." And best of all, we can spend as much time with our dear Lord as we want. He never tires of listening to us – and we feel so much better after the conversation.

When can we begin our group study? I wish I knew. In spite of the so called 'opening up' of Florida, most of us fall into the category of seniors (Not sure I like that word, folks). But as we continue to pray for just such a time, the answer will come.

James 1:12 "Blessed is the one who perseveres under trial because having stood the test, that person will receive the crown of life that the Lord has promised to those who love Him."

The hymn this week was written by Russell Carter in 1886. Carter was a professor in the Pennsylvania Military College of Chester, was a preacher for the Episcopal Church, and later studied medicine becoming a doctor as well as a writer after his health began to fail. He was quite active in meetings and revivals and our hymn this week is a well-known one full of enthusiastic faith and reassurance. Let us sing.

~

STANDING ON THE PROMISES

> (Verse 1)
> *Standing on the promises of Christ, my*
>   *King,*
> *Through eternal ages let his praises ring;*
> *Glory in the highest, I will shout and sing,*
> *Standing on the promises of God.*

(Refrain)
Standing, standing,
Standing on the promises of God, my
    Savior;
Standing, standing,
I'm standing on the promises of God.

(Verse 2)
Standing on the promises that cannot fail.
When the howling storms of doubt and
    fear assail,
By the living Word of God I shall prevail,
Standing on the promises of God.
    [Refrain]

(Verse 3)
Standing on the promises of Christ, the
    Lord,
Bound to him eternally by love's strong
    cord,
Overcoming daily with the Spirit's sword,
Standing on the promises of God.
    [Refrain]

(Verse 4)
Standing on the promises I cannot fall,

List'ning ev'ry moment to the Spirit's call,
Resting in my Savior as my all in all,
Standing on the promises of God.
    [Refrain]

∽

May the Lord bless you and keep you. May the Lord make His face to shine upon you and be gracious to you. May the Lord lift up His countenance upon you and give you peace.

Rich blessings to all. In Christian love,
    Betty & Norman

WEEK TEN

May 12, 2020

Good morning to our dear friends in His name,

It is said that the BOOK OF PROVERBS was written primarily for the younger members of Israel. We understand that the Proverbs were to show them how wisdom can be practically applied to everyday life. The words were meant to assist younger people in avoiding a life of crime, perhaps to avoid gangs and other unsavory ways.

When we see the news today of the actions of the young, we can certainly see what happens when they have been neglected in their preparation for adulthood.

And we – society – are responsible. We have allowed the so-called 'minority', to bring about the changes that we should have contested.

So sorry to speak out loud friends, it is just that I feel for these young people who, through no fault of their own, are committed to this strange way of life that is taking them nowhere. If ever we had a cause to direct our prayers, it should be for them.

PROVERBS 1:8 "Listen my son, to your father's instruction and do not forsake your mothers teaching. They will be a garland to grace your head and a chain to adorn your neck."

PROVERBS 1:10 "My son, if sinners entice you, do not give in to them."

PROVERBS 3:1 "My son, do not forget my teaching, but keep my commands in your heart."

PROVERBS 3:5 "Trust in the Lord with all your heart and lean not on your own understanding."

And so it goes on. We have much enjoyable study ahead of us as we delve into the BOOK OF PROVERBS. Hopefully in the not-too-distant future.

Now for our hymn this week. As I sat in thought of the distressing situations our country is facing, my mind was interrupted by the words of dear Fanny Crosby – "Blessed Assurance, Jesus is Mine", a song she wrote around 1873. Please sing them often in the days and weeks ahead.

~

BLESSED ASSURANCE

(Verse 1)
Blessed assurance, Jesus is mine,
O what a foretaste of glory divine,
Heir of salvation, purchase of God,
Born of His spirit, washed in His blood.

(Refrain)
This is my story, this is my song.
Praising my Savior, all the day long
This is my story, this is my song,
Praising my Savior, all the day long.

(Verse 2)
Perfect submission, all is at rest.
I in my Savior am happy and blest.
Watching and waiting, looking above,
Filled with His goodness, lost in His love.
[Refrain]

∼

May you all be filled with His goodness and lost in His love.

Rich blessings to all,
    Betty & Norman

WEEK ELEVEN

May 19, 2020

*G*ood morning, dear friends,

I had to put on my thinking cap for this week's letter. There is a danger of becoming insular as we endure the 'lock down' from society as we know and miss it. I thought of Luba and tried her method of "Just open the Bible and there is the answer." Thank you, Luba. I opened our huge family Bible and began to read from St. Mathew. And then, I looked at Reverend John

Brown's interpretation and I so enjoyed his words when I read:

> "No place on earth can shut us out from the visits of divine grace. And often the sweetest communion with God is when we are most withdrawn from the world. But what delight Jesus took to fulfill all righteousness required from God, as our surety, and to honor all His Father's institutions. May my soul therefor entertain the most exalted and endearing thoughts of Him, as the Son of God and my Savior, in whom I am accepted to eternal life."

The Reverend John Brown I refer to is the creator of The Self Interpreting Bible printed around 1750. What a remarkable man he was, I ask you to take a moment and let your thoughts take you to this great Theologian with pen in hand, working by the light of a candle almost three hundred years ago to bring us these beautiful interpretations of the Scriptures.

This week's hymn, "Love Divine, All Loves Excelling", is by Charles Wesley. He was the eighteenth child of the Wesleys who lived about ten miles from our home in England. Their 16th century home is still there. It is also quite possible that Rev. Brown and Charles Wesley met in the 1750's as they both moved around England.

You can sing this hymn to two different tunes – both great and both very popular. It's your choice. "Beecer" by Jong Zundel or "Hyfrydol" by Welshman Rowland Prichard.

~

LOVE DIVINE, ALL LOVES EXCELLING

(Verse 1)
Love divine all loves excelling,
Joy of heaven to earth come down.
Fix in us Thy humble dwelling,
All Thy faithful mercies crown.
Jesus, Thou art all compassion,
Pure unbounded love Thou art.
Visit us with Thy salvation,
Enter every trembling heart.

(Verse 2)
Breathe, O breathe Thy loving spirit,
Into every troubled breast.
Let us all in Thee inherit,
Let us find the promised rest.
Take away our bent to sinning,
Alpha and Omega be,

End of faith, as it's beginning,
Set our hearts at liberty.

(Verse 3)
Finish then Thy new creation;
Pure and spotless let us be,
Let us see Thy great salvation
Perfectly restored in Thee.
Changed from glory into glory
Till in heaven we take our place,
Till we cast our crowns before Thee,
Lost in wonder, Love, and praise.

Amen.

~

In His divine all excelling love,
    Betty & Norman

WEEK TWELVE

May 26, 2020

*H*ello, dear friends in Christ,

Welcome to week twelve and Betty is still baking! Yesterday it was English Tea Cakes spread with butter and homemade strawberry jam.

Let me begin in patriotic mode with a couple of words by George Washington concerning the Constitution. He said, "Let us raise a standard in which the wise and honest can repair. The event is in the hands of God." Also, "Of all the dispositions and habits which lead to political prosperity, religion and morality are indispensable supports."

I am sure that over the past months quite a number of sermons have been titled something like "Would Jesus wear a mask?" and the question does bear out the facts of the trials that we are undergoing. It began, I'm sure, that we chose to wear a mask for our own preservation, but then we started to hear the medical staff telling us that it also helps prevent the spread of infection to others. It would seem that there would be no end to the pandemic if we continued to pass the virus from one to another.

I saw one phrase that read, "If we have the faith we profess to have, then we must prioritize LOVE over LIBERTY. We are not just saving ourselves; we are respecting the lives of others. Jesus would have led the way in such a pandemic, by wearing a mask."

As some of you know, I happen to be a lover of poetry. The written rhyming words of the great poets have long had a fascination for me, and the same can be said for the words of every Hymnal. With that in mind, I chose "Master, speak! Thy Servant Heareth", a poem by Frances Havergal who was the daughter of a minister. At age fifteen she gave her life to her Lord with these beautiful words, "I committed my soul to the Savior, and earth and heaven seemed brighter from that moment."

MASTER, SPEAK! THY SERVANT HEARETH

(Verse 1)
Master, speak! Thy servant heareth,
Waiting for Thy gracious word.
Longing for Thy voice that cheereth,
    Master.
Let it now be heard.
I am listening Lord for Thee,
What hast Thou to say to me.

(Verse 2)
Speak to me by name O Master,
Let me know it is to me'
Speak that I may follow faster,
With a step more firm and free.
Where the shepherd leads the flock,
In the shadow of the rock.

(Verse 3)
Master, speak! Though least and lowest.
Let me not unheard depart,
Master, speak! For oh, Thou knowest,
All the yearning of my heart,

Knowest all its truest needs, Speak!
And make me blest indeed.

(Verse 4)
Master speak! And make me ready,
When Thy voice is truly heard,
With obedience glad and steady,
Still to follow every word.
I am listening Lord for Thee, Master,
Speak, oh speak to me.

Amen.

∼

What a pleasure it is to speak to you all every week through the 'magic' of the internet. But in person would be so much better!

Praying for that day and for each one of you.

Rich blessings,
 Betty & Norman

WEEK THIRTEEN

June 2, 2020

Good morning, brothers and sisters in Christ,

Betty and I had a lovely surprise yesterday. We attended church with our son Daryl and his family in Mooresville in North Carolina – through the computer! The surprise, was the service opened and closed with me singing "Sweet Spirit". Our granddaughter – a computer whizz – who creates the transmission each week for their church, had taken one of my recordings and built it into the service. This grand hymn expresses in simple terms the Holy Spirit as it works in the life of the church. It is a fitting hymn wherever God's people gather to worship.

The writer, Doris Mae Akers, was a choir director and one Sunday morning after rehearsal, told her singers that they were not ready to go into the church. They had prayed, but Doris didn't think they had prayed enough. She told them that "Prayer is more important than great voices." They all prayed again with renewed vigor. After which, Doris said to her choir members, "I hate to leave this room because there is such a sweet, sweet Spirit in this place."

The phrase stayed with Doris and she wrote the song the next day. Doris said she was inspired by the words of MATHEW 3:16-17 "And Jesus, when He was baptized, went up straightway out of the water; and, lo, the heavens were opened unto Him, and He saw the spirit of God descending like a dove and lighting upon Him. And lo a voice from heaven saying, 'This is my beloved Son, in whom I am well pleased.'" And, she wrote the line, "Sweet heavenly dove." The text focuses on the baptism of Jesus when "He saw the Spirit of God descending like a dove, and lighting upon Him: And low a voice from heaven saying, 'This, is my beloved Son, in whom I am well pleased.'"

In my 'traveling' days, I was proud to open every

"Sermon in Song" recital with the grand hymn "Sweet, Sweet Spirit" by Doris Mae Akers and I encourage you all to give it a listen. Today's hymn, however, is "Sweet Hour of Prayer" written by W. W. Walford, a blind preacher in England of obscure birth and no education, but of a strong faith.

∼

SWEET HOUR OF PRAYER

> (Verse 1)
> *Sweet hour of prayer! Sweet hour of prayer!*
> *That calls me from a world of care,*
> *And bids me at my Father's throne*
> *Make all my wants and wishes known.*
> *In seasons of distress and grief,*
> *My soul has often found relief,*
> *And oft escaped the tempter's snare*
> *By thy return, sweet hour of prayer!*

> (Verse 2)
> *Sweet hour of prayer! Sweet hour of prayer!*
> *The joys I feel, the bliss I share*

Of those whose anxious spirits burn
With strong desires for thy return!
With such I hasten to the place
Where God my Savior shows His face,
And gladly take my station there,
And wait for thee, sweet hour of prayer!

(Verse 3)
Sweet hour of prayer! Sweet hour of prayer!
Thy wings shall my petition bear
To Him whose truth and faithfulness
Engage the waiting soul to bless.
And since He bids me seek His face,
Believe His word, and trust His grace,
I'll cast on Him my every care,
And wait for thee, sweet hour of prayer!

∼

Blessings dear friends by the sweet, sweet Spirit. Let the peace of Christ rule in your hearts. Amen.

Betty & Norman

WEEK FOURTEEN

June 9, 2020

Good morning, dear friends,

How Betty and I miss your smiling faces.

Let me start this morning with a question. WHAT IS A PROVERB?

My trusty old Oxford dictionary says…'**Proverb**' – a short saying – but full of meaning! The originators were considered to be the fount of wisdom and it is from Solomon and others, that we are fortunate to have a whole book in the Bible to bring us the words of wisdom to enhance our Christian conduct.

My grandmother had a favorite saying that she would tell me: "Aye my lad, there's many a slip twixt the cup and the lip." As a boy, I thought she made it up, then later found it to be from the earliest Greek Mythology. My mother often used, "Easier said than done." Which still didn't always stop me – I guess I had to learn the hard way!

My dad's mother used a saying that bothered me as a boy. When discussing someone's misdeeds she would say, "He's born but he's not dead yet." Which I interpreted as the person concerned still had time to face the results of his actions.

Our study guide begins with PROVERBS 9, but I found PROVERBS 1:7 to be a powerful statement and a good opener. "The fear of the Lord is the beginning of knowledge, but fools despise and instruction." To which Rev. Brown answers, "It is necessary, that everyone who desires true wisdom should begin with, and study, the saving knowledge of God, because without this, all other knowledge is vain and useless." To which we can all say AMEN.

I chose a hymn this week by Robert Robinson, born in 1735. He was an apprentice hairdresser in London. At 17, he was so moved by a sermon on "The wrath to come" that he gave himself to God and a life of religion. As evidence of his devotion, he was moved to express himself with a beautiful poem dedicated to his Savior. As a side note, a poet is described as "Someone with high powers of expression." You can enjoy the expression felt by Robert Robinson in the hymn, "Mighty God, While Angels Bless Thee".

MIGHTY GOD, WHILE ANGELS BLESS THEE

(Verse 1)
Mighty God, while Angels bless Thee,
May a mortal lisp Thy name,
Lord of men as well as Angels,
Thou art every creature's theme.
Lord of every land and nation,
Ancient of eternal days
Sounded through the wide creation,
Be Thou just and endless praise.

(Verse 2)
For the grandeur of Thy nature,
Grand beyond a Seraphs thought.
For the wonders of creation,

Works with skill and kindness wrought.
For Thy providence that governs,
Through Thine Empires wide domain,
Wings an Angel, guides a sparrow.
Blessed be Thy gentle Reign.

(Verse 3)
From the highest throne of glory,
To the cross of deepest woe,
Thou didst stoop to ransom captives,
Flow my praise, forever flow
Re- ascend immortal Savior,
Leave Thy footstool, take Thy throne.
Thence return and reign forever,
Be the kingdom all Thine own.

Rich blessings to each, and every one of you faithful friends.

Betty & Norman

WEEK FIFTEEN

June 16, 2020

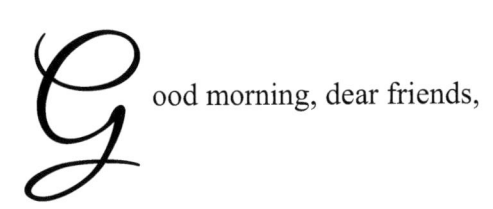

*G*ood morning, dear friends,

We pray our words find you well.

This beautiful country that we are fortunate enough to call home has been fraught, just as many countries, with the virus situation for a year now. The effect on our lives has caused so many problems for people throughout the world. Such activities certainly test our day-to-day living resulting in some difficult times for all ages. In other words, it has been a testing time for all levels of our society. But! There is an answer, and we have it when we turn our thoughts to our Christian hymnal. How fortunate we are to have hundreds of musical prayers available to us just at the turn of a page in our hymnals. And that is just what I did again this week.

However, before the hymn, I was drawn to the words of the Serenity Prayer by Reinhold Neibuhr. He first wrote it as part of a sermon he was to deliver to the Heath Evangelical Union Church in Massachusetts in 1932. Some twenty years later he rewrote the first line to add the word 'Grace' as in this version:

～

SERENITY PRAYER

> "God grant me the serenity to accept the things I cannot change; Courage to change the things I can; And wisdom to know the difference. Living one day at a time; Enjoying one moment at a time; Accepting hardships as the pathway to peace; Taking, as He did, this sinful world as it is, not as I would have it; Trusting that He will make all things right if I surrender to His will; SO that I may be reasonably

happy in this life and supremely happy with Him forever and ever in the next. Amen."

∽

One of the beautiful blessings Christians have is to let the Word of God fill our hearts with grace. The enjoyment of God throughout history has been through singing hymns of praise. The word "**hymn**" derives from Greek ὕμνος (hymnos), which means "a song of praise" and Luther B. Bridgers provides us with the opportunity to do just that this week with his great hymn "He Keeps Me Singing". By the way friends, Luther's eleventh great grandfather was the vicar of St. John the Evangelist in England around the year 1600.

I pray these God-given words will fill your heart as you sing.

∽

HE KEEPS ME SINGING

>(Verse 1)
>*There's within my heart a melody,*
>*Jesus whispers sweet and low*
>*"Fear not I am with thee, peace be still"*

In all of life's ebb and flow.

(Refrain)
Jesus, Jesus, Jesus,
Sweetest name I know.
Fills my every longing,
Keeps me singing as I go.

(Verse 2)
Feasting on the riches of His grace,
Resting neath His sheltering wing.
Always looking on His smiling face,
That is why I shout and sing.

∽

Have a blessed week dear friends as you live in His name.

Christian love to all,
    Betty & Norman

WEEK SIXTEEN

June 23, 2020

*G*ood morning, friends in His special name,

Finally, the talked about book about my family's history is finished. One more proof reading (Betty is my proof reader – and a very good one too) and then it will be ready for publication. More news on this later.

As I looked for my letter content this week, I came across a lady called Luisa M. R. Stead. There is not a lot written about her but I found her faith remained infallible despite very difficult circumstances. And then I remembered a short sentence I wrote in the Foreword to my book: "The reader will discover that although times were occasionally difficult, we were always supported by our beliefs and faith in God."

For some reason, I got stuck on the word '**Hope**' this past week. Experiencing the state of America (according to the news) tends to put the topic of hope (or lack thereof) on our minds. And so, I opened my Oxford dictionary and read, "Hope is expectation and desire combined." Also, "Hope is a feeling of trust." So our hope is and must be in Jesus our Savior.

Hope and confidence is ours when we read passages like the following:

JOHN 6:47 "Verily, verily, I say unto you. He that believeth on me hath everlasting life."

PSALM 3:3 "But Thou, O Lord art a shield for me; my glory, and the lifter up of mine head. I cried unto the Lord with my voice, and He heard me out of His holy hill. I laid me down and slept; I awakened; for the Lord sustained me."

. . .

PHILIPPIANS 3:13-14 "But this is one thing I do, forgetting those things which are behind, and reaching forth unto those things which are before. I press toward the mark of the prize of the high calling of God in Christ Jesus."

And now back to Louisa Stead, a strong committed Christian. Louisa, her husband, and young daughter were on a picnic by the river when her husband dove into the water to attempt to save a small boy from drowning. Tragically, he and the boy went to their deaths. It was years later as once again the memories of that sad day came to mind that Louisa prayerfully penned the words to "'Tis so Sweet to Trust in Jesus."

As you sing, hum, or quietly read this wonderful prayer in the form of a hymn, know that we live through our hope and trust in our given Lord.

∼

'TIS SO SWEET TO TRUST IN JESUS

> (Verse 1)
> *Tis so sweet to trust in Jesus,*
> *And to take Him at His word;*
> *Just to rest upon His promise,*
> *And to know; thus saith the Lord.*

(Refrain)
Jesus, Jesus, how I trust Him!
How I've proved Him o'er and o'er.
Jesus, Jesus, precious Jesus!
O for grace to trust Him more!

(Verse 2)
Yes 'tis sweet to trust in Jesus,
Just from sin and self to cease;
Just from Jesus simply taking,
Life and rest, and joy and peace.

(Verse 3)
I'm so glad I learned to trust Thee,
Precious Jesus, Savior, Friend;
And I know that Thou art with me,
Wilt be with me to the end.

Amen.

∼

Have a wonderful week our dear friends in His name – the only way to live.

    Betty & Norman

WEEK SEVENTEEN

June 30, 2020

Good morning, dear friends in Christ,

Well, there went another week of near isolation for us all. Somehow, Betty and I seem to stay busy from day to day. I must admit that we do spend a lot of time on the phone and, thanks to Skype, the phone bills are quite reasonable. And that is a small price to pay for the communication we enjoy with friends near and far.

I found a couple of poems this week that I thought

you may enjoy. The first one was written by Elizabeth Dorney one hundred years ago. It is a lengthy poem but I thought some of the problems of today aren't really new, and that is evidenced by the first and last verses of "The Chemistry of Character".

∼

THE CHEMISTRY OF CHARACTER

> John and Peter and Robert and Paul,
> God in His wisdom created them all.
> John was a statesman and Peter a slave,
> Robert a preacher and Paul was a knave.
> Evil or good as the case might be,
> White or colored or bond or free,
> John and Peter and Robert and Paul—
> God in His wisdom created them all.
>
> John may in goodness and wisdom
>   increase,
> Peter rejoice in infinite peace;
> Robert may learn that the truths of
>   the Lord
> Are more in the spirit and less in the
>   word;

> And Paul may be blessed with a holier birth
> Than the passions of men had allowed him on earth.
> John and Peter and Robert and Paul—
> God in His wisdom created them all.

∼

The second poem was written by Horatius Bonar, a pastor born in Scotland in 1808. "I Heard the Voice of Jesus Say" touches on loneliness and the hope we have in Jesus Christ. Considering the trying circumstances of today with this pandemic, these lines of verse feel particularly encouraging.

∼

I HEARD THE VOICE OF JESUS SAY

> I heard the voice of Jesus say,
> "Come unto me and rest.
> Lay down, O weary one,
> Lay down your head upon my breast."
> I came to Jesus as I was,
> So weary, worn, and sad.

I found Him in a resting place,
And He has made me glad.

I heard the voice of Jesus say,
"Behold, I freely give
The living water, thirsty one;
Stoop down and drink and live."
I came to Jesus, and I drank
Of that life-giving stream.
My thirst was quenched, my soul revived,
And now I live in Him.

I heard the voice of Jesus say,
"I am the dawning light.
Look unto me, your morn shall rise,
And all your day be bright."
I looked to Jesus, and I found
In Him my star, my sun,
And in that light of life I'll walk
Till trav'ling days are done.

∾

Our hymn this week was written by an Englishman named James Rowe (pseudonym James S. Apple), at least that is where he was born. He came to America in 1890.

He began writing hymns and poetry in 1896 and we can now sing one of his best: "Love Lifted Me".

~

LOVE LIFTED ME

>(Verse 1)
>*I was sinking deep in sin, far from the peaceful shore,*
>*Very deeply stained within, sinking to rise no more.*
>*But the Master of the sea, heard my despairing cry.*
>*From the waters lifted me, now safe am I.*
>
>(Refrain)
>*Love lifted me, Love lifted me,*
>*When nothing else could help,*
>*Love lifted me*
>
>(Verse 2)
>*All my heart to Him I give, ever to Him I'll cling.*
>*In His blessed presence live, ever His praises sing,*

*Love so mighty and so true, merits my
 soul's best songs,
Faithful, Loving service too, to Him
 belongs.*

∼

In His precious name,
 Betty & Norman

WEEK EIGHTEEN

∞

July 7, 2020

*G*ood morning, dear friends in His name, the name of all names,

We do trust that you are all well and getting your vaccine – 'jabs' as they call them in England. Why 'jab' we don't know. A vaccination sounds so much more acceptable, particularly if you don't like needles. And here's a smile for you from our friend Ruth Simko. Ruth was at her doctor's office and saw a sign which said, "Wash your hands and say your Prayers. Because Jesus and germs are everywhere!"

And speaking of Jesus, I quote JOHN 10:27-30 "My sheep hear my voice, and I know them, and they follow me: And I give unto them eternal life; and they shall never perish, neither shall any man pluck them out of my hand. My Father, which gave them me, is greater than all; and no man is able to pluck them out of my Father's hand. I and my Father are one."

Hymns are and always have been, such wonderful instruments of the Glory of God. To most of us, singing hymns was the first thing we remember from out childhood introduction to our church life. They provide an opportunity for a congregation to sing together in Christian worship – what a beautiful sound from a full church.

There is one hymn that always will bring out the best in all of us as we sing and that is "How Great Thou Art". Perhaps because it allows us to express ourselves for all the wonders that our God has provided in one song. And that song had a most interesting beginning.

It started out as a poem by the Reverend Carl Boberg as he attempted to express his life in the Swedish countryside where he lived. He called the poem "O Store Gud" (O Great God).

In 1907, Manfred von Glehn, translated it into his native German. Five years later, in 1912, a Russian Pastor, translated it into Russian. E. Gustav Johnson wrote the first literal English translation, "O Great God", in 1925 though the popular version most sung today was translated by Stuart K. Hine.

In 1922, the hymn was discovered by an English couple, Mr. & Mrs. Stuart Hine, Methodist missionaries from England, who were serving in the Ukraine. Stuart began to translate the hymn into English and added several new phrases in his interpretation. When war broke out in 1939, the Hines were forced to head back to England where the hymn rested until Stuart added one more verse before having the words published. In 1954, his hymn was titled "How Great Thou Art". In the same year, a copy was handed to a member of the Billy Graham crusade team and dear friends, as they say, the rest is history.

I feel sure I don't need to suggest you sing this one as you move around the house. Just let it go, sing from your heart, your neighbors will love it too! Feel free to sing Hine's more popular translation or E. Gustav Johnson's earlier translation, the first English literal translation of Boberg's poem:

~

O MIGHTY GOD

> (Verse 1)
> *O mighty God, when I behold the wonder*
> *Of nature's beauty, wrought by words of*
> *Thine,*
> *And how Thou leadest all from realms up*
> *yonder,*
> *Sustaining earthly life in love benign*
>
> (Refrain)
> *With rapture filled, my soul Thy name*
> *would laud,*
> *O mighty God! O mighty God!*
> *With rapture filled, my soul Thy name*
> *would laud,*
> *O mighty God! O mighty God!*
>
> (Verse 4)
> *When, crushed by guilt of sin, before Him*
> *kneeling*
> *I plead for mercy and for grace and peace,*
> *I feel His balm and all my bruises healing,*
> *He saves my soul and sets my heart at*
> *ease.* [Refrain]

(Verse 5)
When finally the mists of time have vanished,
And I in truth my faith confirmed shall see,
Upon the shores where earthly ills are banished,
I enter, Lord, to dwell in peace with Thee.
[Refrain]

Amen.

~

Well dear friends, whether you sang or just read the words, you have thanked our precious Father from the heights to the very depths. And know He heard you!

Betty & Norman

WEEK NINETEEN

July 14, 2020

Good morning, dear friends in love and worship,

Is it just me, or did last week go faster than usual? Perhaps just wishful thinking and hoping to get back to normal – although I keep hearing "What is normal anymore?" My answer is, "Life is normal when we give thanks to our Lord and Savior and in turn, show love for one another." And that says it all in my book.

And on the subject of 'saying it all', my choice of a

hymn this week is a good example. The first verse is so beautifully inclusive, it says all we ever need to know about our Christian lives, and is the composer's interpretation of PSALM 90.

The author, Isaac Watts was born in England in 1674 and even in his childhood began to write rhymes (they used to be called rimes). He laughed out loud one evening during family prayers. When asked why, he claimed to have seen a mouse run up the bell rope by the fireplace which prompted him to write "A mouse for want of better stairs, ran up a rope to say his prayers."

By the way, in those early days, the only songs permitted in church were rhyming versions of the PSALMS. The custom was for the cleric to read a line of the hymn, then the congregation sang that line and waited for him to read the next line. Going to church could be a lengthy experience, but there was no rushing home to see the ball game on TV in those days.

The music to our hymn this week, "O God, Our Help in Ages Past", was composed eleven years before Watts wrote the words, which makes us think how divinely inspired the words and music proved to be.

O GOD, OUR HELP IN AGES PAST

(Verse 1)
O God, our help in ages past,
Our hope for years to come.
Our shelter from the stormy blast,
And our eternal home.

(Verse 2)
Under the shadow of Thy throne
Thy Saints have dwelt secure.
Sufficient is Thine arm alone
And our defense is sure.

(Verse 3)
Before the hills in order stood,
Or earth received her frame,
From everlasting Thou art God,
To endless years the same.

(Verse 4)
A thousand ages in Thy sight,
Are like an evening gone:
Short as the watch that ends the night,
Before the rising sun.

(Verse 5)
O God, our help in ages past,
Our hope for years to come.
Be Thou our guide while life shall last,
And our eternal home.

∾

Thanks to Isaac Watts for creating such a wonderful interpretation of the words of Moses – truly a man of God.

Yours, dear friends in love and peace,
    Betty & Norman

WEEK TWENTY

July 21, 2020

Good morning, our friends in the Lord,

We do trust that you are all well and safe from the virus as the isolation continues. They used to talk about prisoners going "stir crazy" and after this past year I think we understand what they meant! But, what a joy to know that we have Jesus with us in difficult times. Amen.

It is true, that our long habit of gathering to worship together and sing His praises is what so many of us have missed. We read of Paul in COLOSSIANS 3:16 telling us to "Let the word of Christ dwell in you richly in all wisdom; teaching and admonishing one another in Psalms and Hymns and spiritual songs. Singing with grace in your hearts to the Lord." PSALM 92 is titled "A Psalm or song for the Sabbath Day" and says, "It is a good thing to give thanks unto the Lord, and to sing praises unto Thy name, O most high." Having said that, we may not gather to sing together, but as we sing at home, let us all remember the joyful endings to our Tara Woods gatherings.

I have chosen a favorite for us this week that really did begin life as a poem. Its writer, Henry van Dyke, was a Presbyterian and excelled as a poet. He served as a professor of English Literature at Princeton. He also was elected by President Woodrow Wilson to become Minister to the Netherlands and Luxembourg. He also wrote in 1907, the poem "Hymn to Joy". He decided to set the words to a piece of music by Ludwig van Beethoven – the "Ode to Joy" movement of his Ninth Symphony. This massive work by one of the greatest composers ever, proved to be the ideal setting for that wonderful hymn "Joyful, Joyful We Adore Thee".

I can only say that Henry van Dyke must have encountered situations in his life that probably mirror the circumstances we have witnessed over the past year. But, do dwell on the words as you read the hymn, and let them truly lift you to the joy divine.

Just as a point of interest, Beethoven never got to hear his great work, the Ninth Symphony, performed. Oh, he was at the performance, but by then his hearing had worsened to the point that he was deaf. The poor chap couldn't hear the thunderous applause of the audience after it was over.

∽

JOYFUL, JOYFUL, WE ADORE THEE

> (Verse 1)
> *Joyful, joyful, we adore Thee, God of*
> *   Glory, Lord of Love*
> *Hearts unfold like flowers before Thee,*
> *   Opening to the sun above,*
> *Melt the clouds of sin and sadness, Drive*
> *   the dark of doubt away.*
> *Giver of immortal gladness, Fill us with*
> *   the light of day.*
>
> (Verse 2)
> *All Thy works with joy surround Thee,*
> *   Earth and heaven reflect Thy rays,*

*Stars and Angels sing around Thee, Center
of unbroken praise.
Field and forest vale and mountain,
Flowery meadow flashing sea.
Chanting bird and flowing fountain, Call
us to rejoice in Thee.*

(Verse 3)
*Thou art giving and forgiving. Ever
blessing, ever blest,
Well spring of the joy of living, Ocean
depth of rest!
Thou our Father, Christ our Brother - All
who live in love are Thine;
Teach us how to love each other, Lift us to
the joy divine.*

(Verse 4)
*Mortals join the mighty chorus Which the
morning stars began,
Father love is reigning o'er us, Brother
love binds man to man.
Ever singing march we onward, Victors in
the midst of strife;
Joyful music leads us sunward in the
triumph song of life.*

Amen. Have a blessed week, dear friends, with the assurance of the words from 2 TIMOTHY 1:7 "For God hath not given us the spirit of fear; but of power and of love, and of a sound mind." Amen.

In love and in His precious name,
    Betty & Norman

WEEK TWENTY-ONE

July 28, 2020

*G*ood morning, dear friends,

What a beautiful morning it is with three rabbits chasing around the garden, four ducks here for their morning snack, and a host of birds gathered at the bird feeder. The sort of morning God intended to give us thoughts for the day.

And now for a story. When I retired (28 years ago), Betty and I decided to spend more time in England so off we went for the summer of 1993. Our first Sunday there, knowing there is no Presbyterian church anymore, we opted for another local church – the Ackworth Methodist Church in the village – and walked in to find another church family! Just entering the front door we were warmly greeted and that continued before and after the service. It seemed like everyone stayed for coffee just to welcome the Joneses! And that wonderful welcome has never worn out! That loving Christian spirit has been a large part of our annual pilgrimage to Yorkshire ever since.

We send our weekly letter to a couple of friends in Ackworth and one of them is a Methodist minister – dear Ruth Miles. After last week's letter, Ruth was kind enough to share a hymn that was new to us – but it tells a story of the joy of singing praises to Him who is above all. Ruth is acquainted with the composer, Brian Hoare, who is also a Methodist minister. He tells of writing the hymn while on a train journey to London and he also composed the music which he calls 'Chatsworth'. Ruth refers to it as a 'modern' hymn which tells of the reasons why we should sing out loud. You may not be familiar with the tune, but you can find it online by searching for "Born in Song" by Brian Hoare.

And Ruth comments, "A lovely hymn that reminds us, that even in the pandemic, all power is given to our

Lord and He is always with us and the hope of every believer – song will continue when this life is over." To which, we say, "Amen!"

Following that thought, I would like to introduce "Sing to the Lord a Joyful Song" as our hymn for this week. It was written by John Monsell, an Irishman educated at Trinity College in Dublin. Monsell enjoyed not only serving in several churches in both Ireland and England, but also found a great joy in composing poetry and hymns. This particular hymn of his is a celebration of song and an encouragement to sing – something I think you might appreciate well.

~

SING TO THE LORD A JOYFUL SONG

Sing to the Lord a joyful song,
Lift up your hearts, your voices raise;
To us His gracious gifts belong,
To Him our songs of love and praise.

For life and love, for rest and food,
For daily help and nightly care,
Sing to the Lord, for He is good,
And praise His name, for it is fair.

For strength to those who on Him wait,
His truth to prove, His will to do,
Sing to our God, for He is great,
Trust in His name, for it is true.

∽

Thank you, Ruth, and blessings and love to all.
    Betty & Norman

WEEK TWENTY-TWO

August 4, 2020

*G*ood morning, dear loving Christian friends,

This year, unfortunately, saw the cancellation of our family escape to the woods. The 'woods' being our Presbyterian Retreat – Cedarkirk – about 120 miles north of Fort Myers, Florida. Customarily, a dozen or more of our family enjoy a wonderful weekend and really is located deep in the woods with a beautiful river running through. An absolute haven of rest and relaxation for all ages. Our open-air service on Sunday morning is on a grassy slope with the 'tree' cross at the bottom. Last year, as we prayed and sang with gusto, a lovely bright Red Cardinal bird appeared, he just sat and listened. He may have heard better singing but when we take time to pray and sing in the quiet sounds of nature, we can be sure God is in our midst. We felt sure that we heard Him whisper "Peace." Amen.

Which brings me to the wonders that we experience when we feel that God is always with and around us in all times to support and encourage us, and I quote from the following:

PROVERBS 3:5-6 "Trust in the Lord with all your heart, and do not lean upon your own understanding. In all your ways acknowledge Him, and He will make straight your paths."

PSALMS 23:4 "Even though I walk through the valley of the shadow of death, I will fear no evil, for You are with me, Your rod and Your staff, they comfort me."

. . .

Isaiah 41:10 "Fear not for I am with you; be not dismayed, for I am your God; I will strengthen you, I will help you, I will uphold you with my righteous right hand."

And speaking of strength, how about this for a statement by Fannie Crosby, undoubtably the most prolific hymn writer ever: "It seemed intended by the blessed providence of God, that I should be blind all my life, and I thank Him for the dispensation. If perfect earthly sight were offered me tomorrow, I would not accept it. I might not have sung hymns to the praise of God if I had been distracted by the beautiful and interesting things about me." This amazing lady also said, "When I get to heaven, the first face that shall ever gladden my sight will be that of my Savior."

No wonder, that with such complete faith, Fannie could write this week's hymn.

ALL THE WAY MY SAVIOR LEADS ME

(Verse 1)
All the way, my Savior leads me,
What have I to ask beside?
Can I doubt His tender mercy,

Who through life has been my guide.
Heavenly peace, divinest comfort.
Here by faith in Him to dwell!
For I know what e're befall me,
Jesus doeth all things well.

(Verse 2)
All the way my Savior leads me;
Cheers each winding path I tread.
Gives me grace for every trial.
Feeds me with the living bread;
Though my weary steps may falter,
And my soul a thirst may be,
Gushing from the rock before me,
Lo! a spring of joy I see.

(Verse 3)
All the way my Savior leads me;
Oh, the fullness of His love!
Perfect rest to me is promised
In my Father's house above;
When my spirit, clothed immortal,
Wings its flight to realms of day,
This my song through endless ages;
Jesus led me all the way.

*Don't forget to repeat the last line of each verse!

∽

The Lord is our strength and our salvation.
With our love and His blessing,
Betty & Norman

WEEK TWENTY-THREE

August 11, 2020

Good morning, dear friends of the Tara Woods Bible Study Group,

During our years of Bible study, I have had the good fortune to make another friend namely the Reverend John Brown. You all will remember the times I have mentioned his name and referred to his words from the Self-Interpreting Bible which he authored in 1778. This masterful work came into my family through my Great, Great, Great Grandfather around 1800. This Bible has been in the family for over two hundred years and I have owned it for the past 65 years.

Young John Brown, born in Scotland in 1722, was an orphan at the age of eleven after a very brief education. As a shepherd boy working on a sheep farm, he experienced a Christian conversion and dedicated himself to teaching himself Greek, Latin, and Hebrew. At age 16, he heard that a bookstore in St. Andrews had copies of the Greek New Testament. He walked the 25 miles to the book store and there met a Professor of Greek who said if John could read it he would make him a gift of the book. Read it he did, and walked home with the gift.

Enjoy this special prayer by the Reverend John Brown:

> "Oh! What do I owe to Christ! If I am accepted of God – it is in Him. If I receive the spirit, it is through Him. If I am tempted as a Christian – it is in conformity to Him. If I resist the devil and he flees from me – it is through Him having been tempted that He might rescue those that are tempted. If Angels minister to me – it is at His command and for His sake. If I am called as a Christian or to minister – it is by Him. If I am delivered from disease or devils – I owe all to Him. If I have experienced His Grace, let me gratefully employ all that I have in His service and praise. Amen."

And yet we experience another epoch of the times,

which leaves much consternation in our lives and the lives of others. Invariably, such happenings cause those of us who know and have our trust in our Savior far less concern than those who have still not given their lives over to His protection. I sat this morning in thought when the simple, but so meaningful, words of one of my old favorite songs came to mind. It is called "Enough to Know" written by Frances S. Clark back in 1915.

∼

ENOUGH TO KNOW

(Verse 1)
I know not how, nor when, nor why,
I can but this, on God rely;
His truth, His love eternal flow;
God's Life! It is enough to know.
I rest content what e'er betide,
For love and peace with me abide;
I care not how my footsteps go,
God guides! This enough to know.

(Verse 2)
I know not when I shall forsake all sin,
And in His likeness wake,

> *But to Christ's stature I shall grow,*
> *God reigns! This is enough to know.*
> *I know not why sometimes I fall,*
> *Seem to forget that God is all.*
> *I grasp His outstretched arms and lo,*
> *God is! This is enough to know.*

∾

In PSALM 18, David wrote on the day that he was delivered from his enemies. "I will love Thee, O Lord my strength. The Lord is my rock, and my fortress, and my deliverer; my God, my strength, in whom I will trust. I will call upon the Lord who is worthy to be praised, so shall I be saved from mine enemies."

Blessings and love to all,
    Betty & Norman

WEEK TWENTY-FOUR

August 18, 2020

Good morning, dear friends who live by His word,

This past Sunday, I had the pleasure of singing one of my favorite hymns for our Sunday online service. It is a hymn that I have enjoyed singing for as long as I have known it – and friends, that is a long time! The words by Richard Blanchard so echo the words of our Savior as read in the Book of JOHN 14:13-14 "Jesus answered and said unto her, 'Whosoever drinketh of this water shall thirst again: But whosoever drinketh of the water that I shall give him shall never thirst; but the water that I shall give him shall be in a well of water springing up into everlasting life.'" Friends, what a promise for us to live by. Amen.

I have chosen a few short statements of friends in many lands after they first heard this grand song of worship.

> "I was empty, broken and lost and gave up on the life I was given, I heard this song and not I – but Christ filled my emptiness. So inspiring, having all it takes to fill the spirit."

> "Yes, my cup needed to be filled, not by the earthly treasure which will surely pass away one day, but by the eternal substance only given in Jesus Christ."

Always an assurance to know that when we approach our Savior with our emptiness, we leave filled up to overflowing!

And dear friends, like so many of our great hymns, it has a story behind it. Richard Blanchard, the author, was born in China as the son of a Missionary. He eventually became a Methodist minister and pastored a church in Coral Gables, Florida. One day, he had an appointment with a young couple to discuss their forthcoming wedding. Unfortunately, they failed to show at the appointed time. He informed his secretary to call him when they arrived and headed for his study where he had a piano. Richard sat at the piano with a new song in mind based on JOHN 14:13 and "Fill My Cup, Lord" was the result. Should we feel pleased that the couple failed to show? I encourage you to find a moment today to give this song a listen and, even better, to sing along.

The hymn we shall be singing together today was written in the 1700s by Robert Robinson who was originally apprenticed to a hairdresser. One day he heard a particularly impactful sermon and, after much spiritual wrestling, eventually turned to a religious life. A prayerful poem you may well find familiar, it is called "Come, Thou Fount of Every Blessing".

∿

COME, THOU FOUNT OF EVERY BLESSING

>(Verse 1)
>*Come, thou Fount of every blessing,*
>*Tune my heart to sing thy grace;*
>*Streams of mercy, never ceasing,*
>*Call for songs of loudest praise.*
>*Teach me some melodious sonnet,*
>*Sung by flaming tongues above.*
>*Praise the mount I'm fixed upon it*

Mount of God's redeeming love.

(Verse 2)
Here I find my greatest treasure;
Hither by Thy help I've come;
And I hope by Thy good pleasure,
Safely to arrive at home.
Jesus sought me when a stranger,
Wandering from the fold of God;
He to rescue me from danger,
Bought me with His precious blood.

(Verse 3)
Oh to grace how great a debtor
Daily I'm constrained to be!
Let thy goodness, like a fetter,
Bind my wandering heart to thee
Prone to wander, Lord, I feel it,
Prone to leave the God I love;
Here's my heart, O take and seal it;
Seal it for thy courts above.

∼

Those wonderful words of praise call for a closing from NUMBERS 6:24-26 "The Lord bless you and keep you.

The Lord make His face to shine upon you and be gracious unto you. The Lord lift up His countenance upon you, and give you peace." Amen.

May all your cups be full. Lovingly,
    Betty & Norman

WEEK TWENTY-FIVE

August 26, 2020

*H*ello, dear friends in Christ,

Betty tells me that today was our 148th day in exile!! And I can't say that I am getting used to it – but am putting up with it. I must admit that I have found so much to do between music, genealogy, writing, studying, and some general household chores.

Now about our new books on PROVERBS, we do have them but with our new rules on staying home, it will have to be a little later. However, it would also be good for us to spend some time in preparation because PROVERBS will take some serious, but so informative, study. In fact, I am looking forward to the adventure. In 1 KINGS 4:32 it is said that Solomon spoke three thousand and five words of wisdom to the people of Israel in his efforts to show them how wisdom can be practically applied to their everyday lives. We have a busy time ahead friends.

Speaking of wisdom, let me add a few words on wisdom from my old pal Reverend John Brown when he describes NUMBERS:

> "As the Book of Psalms is calculated to make our hearts warm towards God in Holy and pious affections, the scope of Numbers is to make our face shine before men in a prudent, discreet, honest, and useful conversation; which is a no less necessary part of practical religion. And no book in this world, in so small a compass, affords us such a complete body of rules for directing our personal and relative behavior."

I have spent many hours arranging and sorting out over 50 years of sacred music and remain struck by the beauty of the pairing of the words and music. Perhaps I could include an old favorite of mine by William B. Olds taken from PSALM 107:20.

NORMAN JONES

HE SENT HIS WORD AND HEALED THEM

He sent his word and healed them,
When sorrow bowed them low.
They felt His deep compassion,
Like healing waters flow
O, love past understanding,
Our mortal woes to heal,
That hope of life eternal,
Thou didst to us reveal.

He sent His word and healed them,
When mortal ills prevailed,
The power of God restored them,
When human skill had failed.
God, give us Grace to trust Thee,
Give courage to the soul,
That we may hear Thee saying,
"Thy faith has made thee whole."

And the very last line is what our Christian fellowship is all about:

With our faith we are everything that God intended! Amen.

God bless dear friends,
　　Betty & Norman

WEEK TWENTY-SIX

September 1, 2020

*G*ood morning, dear friends in His name,

If you found yourself with a little extra time on your hands during the past week – we are all in the same club! However, having had a share of the 'news', we found solace in Matthew 5. What marvelous words of encouragement in a few short verses. It is impossible to read verse after verse and not see yourself covered by His Word and the comfort gained is immeasurable. My dictionary says '**Blessedness**' is "enjoyment of Divine favor."

Could we ask for more than His words from the "Sermon on the Mount."

∽

MATTHEW 5:1-14 "Now when Jesus saw the crowds, he went up on a mountainside and sat down. His disciples came to him, and he began to teach them. He said:

"Blessed are the poor in spirit, for theirs is the kingdom of heaven.

Blessed are those who mourn, for they will be comforted.

Blessed are the meek, for they will inherit the earth.

Blessed are those who hunger and thirst for righteousness, for they will be filled.

Blessed are the merciful, for they will be shown mercy.

Blessed are the pure in heart, for they will see God.

Blessed are the peacemakers, for they will be called children of God.

Blessed are those who are persecuted because of righteousness, for theirs is the kingdom of heaven.

Blessed are you when people insult you, persecute you and falsely say all kinds of evil against you because of me. Rejoice and be glad, because great is your reward in heaven, for in the same way they persecuted the prophets who were before you."

∽

To have composed a beautiful anthem for a great nation is an achievement but when we realize that the writer was still in college, it is remarkable. And that brings us to young Samuel Francis Smith. He was studying for the Ministry at the Theological Seminary at Andover, Massachusetts. His friend, Lowell Mason, a musician, had given him a book of German hymns and asked him to see if any of the hymns were suitable for a children's hymn book. One of the tunes which appealed to him turned out to be the music we know as "God Save the King." Although it was new to Samuel at the time, he liked the spirited tempo. He claimed that an air of patriotism ran through his mind as he read the music and on a scrap of paper, he began to write. The whole process took him about a half hour and "America" was born.

Incidentally, the music to "God Save the King" was written around five hundred years ago, possibly by John Bull during the reign of Queen Elizabeth I, but not published until 1744.

This wonderful hymn was actually used as an unofficial National Anthem before the adoption of "The Star-Spangled Banner" in 1931. Now, I hope you are ready to sing, or hum, or just enjoy the words.

∾

AMERICA (MY COUNTRY 'TIS OF THEE)

My country, 'tis of thee,
Sweet land of liberty,
Of thee I sing;
Land where my fathers died,
Land of the pilgrims' pride,
From ev'ry mountainside
Let freedom ring!

My native country, thee,
Land of the noble free,
Thy name I love;
I love thy rocks and rills,
Thy woods and templed hills;
My heart with rapture thrills,
Like that above.

Let music swell the breeze,
And ring from all the trees

Sweet freedom's song;
Let mortal tongues awake;
Let all that breathe partake;
Let rocks their silence break,
The sound prolong.

Our fathers' God to Thee,
Author of liberty,
To Thee we sing.
Long may our land be bright,
With freedom's holy light,
Protect us by Thy might,
Great God our King!

On July 4, 1832, young Samuel was surprised to hear his patriotic hymn sung in public for the first time by a chorus of children in the Park Street Church. In just a few years it was being sung all over the country.

Love to all, as always,
    Betty & Norman

WEEK TWENTY-SEVEN

September 8, 2020

*G*ood morning, dear friends in His name,

We do pray that these words will find you fit and well.

In an idle moment this past week – if you could imagine that – I happened to be reading from my old Church of England Common Prayer book. On page 5, it spells out the "Act for Uniformity of Common Prayer" as prepared for the new Queen Mary when she was crowned in 1553! It spells out every Prayer to be used at every occasion by every serving vicar or any other Minister in every church in the land. It also spells out the penalty if any one of them should change as much as a single word. First offence, one hundred marks ($200,000 today), second offence, $800,000 today, third offence – and this is the big one – LIFE IMPRISONMENT! It sure paid to stick to the rules in those days.

The church Betty and I were attending, which we both attended as children, was still using the same book of Common Prayer until a couple of years ago. Now they refer to the previous book as "The Old One". It took them 500 years to change! Interestingly, we will be using some of the Prayers at our grandson's Baptism in the near future.

And while I have my old English Book of Common Prayer open, I see a "Prayer for the Deliverance From the Plague":

> "We humbly acknowledge before Thee, O most merciful Father, that all the punishments which are threatened in Thy law might justly have fallen upon us, by reason of our manifold transgressions and hardness of heart: Yet seeing that it hath pleased Thee of Thy tender mercy, upon our weak and unworthy humiliation, to assuage the contagious sickness were with we have lately been sore afflicted, and to restore the voice of joy and health into our dwellings; We offer unto Thy divine Majesty the sacrifice of praise

and thanksgiving, lauding and magnifying Thy glorious Name for such Thy preservation and providence over us; through Jesus Christ our Lord, Amen."

This Prayer and others are still in the book listed under "Thanksgiving".

CORINTHIANS 4:5-6 "For we preach not ourselves, but Christ Jesus the Lord; and ourselves your servants for Jesus sake. For God, who commanded the light to shine out of darkness, hath shined in our hearts, to give the light of the knowledge of the glory of God in the face of Jesus Christ." Amen.

This week's hymn was written by Walter Smith back in 1867. He pursued theological studies and was later ordained a pastor of the Scottish Church and also enjoyed penning many a poem including the hymn "Immortal, Invisible."

IMMORTAL, INVISIBLE

Immortal, invisible, God only wise,
In light inaccessible, hid from our eyes,
Most blessed, most glorious, the Ancient of Days,
Almighty, victorious, thy great name we praise.

Unresting, unhasting, and silent as light,
Nor wanting, nor wasting, thou rulest in might,
Thy justice like mountains high soaring above
Thy clouds, which are fountains of goodness and love.

To all, life thou givest, to both great and small.
In all life thou livest, the true life of all.
We blossom and flourish as leaves on the tree,
And wither and perish, but naught changeth thee.

Great God of all glory, great God of all
    light,
Thine angels adore thee, all veiling their
    sight.
All praise we would render; O help us
    to see
'Tis only the splendor of light hideth thee.

∼

Love and blessings,
    Betty & Norman

WEEK TWENTY-EIGHT

⚜

September 15, 2020

*G*ood morning, dear friends in His name,

Week 28, seven months since we had the pleasure of each other's company, which makes us all half a year older. I find it interesting how the media is telling us how bad things are and yet we have more tools for communication than at any time in history. Yet still it is reported that there are many people feeling alone, and that is understandable. BUT there is another way to look at these times. Thanks to our God, we are never alone. We all have one who will never forsake us. Even when no one else knows what we are going through, He knows and He remembers us. He sees us through life's difficult times. He also encourages us to help others, with a smile, a word, or a phone call. The beauty is that when we reach out to others in His name to lift their spirits, we lift our own.

I opened my *Jesus Calling* by Sarah Young for today's reading, a devotional I highly recommend, and today's message spoke on encountering adversity and remembering to place our faith and trust in God in both the good times when life seems easy and the tough times that fill us with fear. Similarly, I'd like to share a poem by Cecil Frances Alexander.

∽

JESUS CALLS US O'ER THE TUMULT

> Jesus calls us o'er the tumult
> Of our life's wild, restless sea;
> Day by day His sweet voice soundeth,
> Saying "Christian, follow me."

As, of old, apostles heard it
By the Galilean lake,
Turned from home and toil and kindred,
Leaving all for His dear sake.

Jesus calls us from the worship
Of the vain world's golden store,
From each idol that would keep us,
Saying "Christian, love me more."

In our joys and in our sorrows,
Days of toil and hours of ease,
Still He calls, in cares and pleasures,
"Christian, love me more than these."

Jesus calls us; by thy mercies,
Savior, may we hear thy call,
Give our hearts to thing obedience,
Serve and love thee best of all.

∼

The words and music to our hymn this week, were written by an Italian Theologian and Musician, Felice De Giardini. They followed a request by the Countess Selina

Shirley, a very wealthy English socialite who built more than 60 Methodist Churches and financed several more. Giardini was a chorister at the Milan Cathedral, but also a very accomplished Violinist who spent most of his adult life in London. He composed 35 hymns but is best remembered for "Come Thou Almighty King".

As you take time to read these wonderful words, I know the tune will come to you.

∾

COME THOU ALMIGHTY KING

(Verse 1)
Come Thou Almighty King,
Help us Thy name to sing.
Help us to praise;
Father! All glorious,
O'er all victorious,
Come and reign over us,
Ancient of days.

(Verse 2)
Come Thou Incarnate Word,
Gird on Thy mighty sword.

Our prayer attend!
Come and Thy people bless,
And give Thy word success,
Spirit of Holiness,
On us descend.

(Verse 3)
Come, Holy comforter,
Thy sacred witness bear.
In this glad hour!
Thou who almighty art,
Now rule in every heart,
And ne'er from us depart,
Spirit of love.

(Verse 4)
To Thee, great One in Three.
The highest praises be,
Hence evermore;
His sovereign majesty
May we in glory see.
And to eternity
Love and adore.

Amen.

What a privilege to carry everything to God in prayer.
    Betty & Norman

WEEK TWENTY-NINE

September 22, 2020

Good morning, dear friends,

Due to the difficult times we are living in, I get to spend a little more time with my poetry books, which I so enjoy. I find that when I get engrossed in words written by others in such beautiful form, I tend to escape – for a brief time – into another world. I thought perhaps these words from the pen of Julian Cutler might do the same for you. As you read his words on the four seasons, read slow and relaxed and let your mind take in the beauty of the countryside and what God has provided for us.

∼

THROUGH THE YEAR

>God be with you in the Springtime,
>>When violets unfold,
>>And the buttercups and cowslips
>>Fill the fields with yellow gold;
>>In the time of apple blossoms
>>When the happy bluebird sings,
>>Filling all the world with gladness –
>>God be with you in the Spring!

>God be with you in the Summer
>>When the sweet June roses blow
>>When the bobolinks are laughing
>>And the brooks with music flow;
>>When the fields are white with daisies
>>And the days are glad and long—
>>God be with you in the Summer,
>>Filling all your world with song.

>God be with you in the Autumn,

NORMAN JONES

> When the birds and flowers have fled,
> And along the woodland pathways
> Leaves are falling, gold and red;
> When the Summer lies behind you,
> In the evening of the year—
> God be with you in the Autumn,
> Then to fill your heart with cheer.

God be with you in the Winter,
> When the snow lies deep and white,
> When the sleeping fields are silent
> And the stars gleam cold and bright.
> When the hand and heart are tired
> With life's long and weary quest—
> God be with you in the Winter,
> Just to guide you into rest.

∼

Let's sing a song of the countryside friends. Cecil Alexander wrote this one:

ALL THINGS BRIGHT AND BEAUTIFUL

> *All things bright and beautiful,*
> *All creatures great and small.*

All things wise and wonderful,
Our Father made them all.
Each little flower that opens,
Each little bird that sings.
He made their glowing colors,
He made their tiny wings.

Cold wind in the winter,
Pleasant summer sun.
Ripe fruits in the garden,
He made them every one.
He gave us eyes to see them,
And lips that we might tell,
How good is God our Father,
Who doeth all things well.

Amen.

With that said, dear friends, all be safe and well.
    In His precious name, God bless.
    Betty & Norman

WEEK THIRTY

September 29, 2020

Good morning, special (and missed) friends,

The announcement this week, that we may now proceed as 'normal', reminded me of times in my youth when the Germans decided to drop bombs around our village. They were really aiming at our local mine because the coal was so important for the factories to keep England going. At the first alarm, we went into the bomb shelters where we stayed, sometimes for several hours, until the 'all clear' alarm sounded. Even then, there were some who just had to be sure that the last German plane had gone. I remember the others encouraging them that it was 'All over'. Then, they reluctantly emerged and went home.

So! Do we or don't we wear our masks and attempt to carry on as normal? But! Don't look at me, because I was probably one of those reluctant to leave the bomb shelter! I am sure there will be more news to follow on the mask subject. Until then, stay safe and well.

Betty and I so enjoyed the Prayer March last Saturday on television. The Graham family did an outstanding job of bringing us something very special from Washington. It should have been mandatory that every member of Congress attend!! Some of the comments were so enlightening such as:

> "This is what Heaven is like – all different people and all focused on prayer."

> "Our battle is done on our knees."

> "Don't forget to listen when you pray."

> "Neighborhoods must have brotherhood."

"Focus on God, not the problems."

...and many more. And then the finale, when all eyes were focused on the Capitol Building as Franklin Graham gave the closing prayers. Quite a morning.

Henry F. Lyte wrote our song this week. A beautiful hymn written mere months before he passed and though some may view this hymn as somber, if you truly listen to the words you can hear the great faith and hope within them. A song of assurance, not of fear!

∼

ABIDE WITH ME

>(Verse 1)
>*Abide with me: fast falls the eventide;*
>*The darkness deepens; Lord, with me abide.*
>*When other helpers fail and comforts flee,*
>*Help of the helpless, O abide with me.*
>
>(Verse 4)
>*I fear no foe with thee at hand to bless,*
>*Ills have no weight, and tears no bitterness.*

Where is death's sting? Where, grave, thy victory?
I triumph still, if thou abide with me.

∾

Till the next time, the Lord bless and keep you.
   In Christian love,
   Betty & Norman

WEEK THIRTY-ONE

October 6, 2020

*D*ear special friends in His name,

God will take care of you! Our letter this week starts as a reminder of our early days in America. We get to sing this grand old hymn later but first we trust that your week has gone well for you as we continue in the 'stay at home/wear your mask' existence. But now—a story.

This week, we celebrated 58 years since we set foot on American soil. We arrived in North Fort Myers with very little money but ready for adventure. We had arranged to spend a few days with a couple we knew, but we also knew that we had to find a home of our own. We decided to buy a mobile home to start. It cost $5,000 — a huge sum at the time — and we were broke with no job in sight!!

On Monday morning, I walked into the First National Bank and met a Loan Officer called Farrell Broyles. When he heard that I had no job and had only been in the States for two weeks, he put down his pen and told me that if he took my request upstairs, I would hear the staff laughing. I looked at him and said that he was dealing with a man of his word and that the bank would never regret making me the loan. He appeared shortly with a check for $5,000!!!

Farrell eventually became the bank President and we actually became friends and played golf together – and the bank never regretted the loan. Betty and I believe that the hand of God was over that bank all those years ago. The mobile home was delivered the very next day and on the next Monday morning I found a job! Our God took good care of us. Amen.

Have you ever had the thought that a certain hymn was written just for you? We think that when that happens, it really was – but you are still glad to share it with others.

We can thank Civilla Martin for these beautiful words. She actually wrote several hundred hymns and religious songs but our song this week happens to be the very first hymn that Civilla wrote. This lady was married to a Baptist minister and travelled with him on evangelistic work. However, because of frail health she was compelled to stay home much of the time. In 1904, she became world famous with her very first hymn – "God Will Take Care of You". Please read, sing along, and know that God is good!

∾

GOD WILL TAKE CARE OF YOU

>(Verse 1)
>*Be not dismayed whate'er betide,*
>*God will take care of you;*
>*Beneath his wings of love abide,*
>*God will take care of you.*

>(Refrain)
>*God will take care of you,*
>*Through ev'ry day, O'er all the way;*
>*He will take care of you,*
>*God will take care of you.*

(Verse 2)
Through days of toil when heart does fail,
God will take care of you;
When dangers fierce your path assail,
God will take care of you. [Refrain]

(Verse 3)
All you may need he will provide,
God will take care of you;
Nothing you ask will be denied,
God will take care of you. [Refrain]

(Verse 4)
No matter what may be the test,
God will take care of you;
Lean, weary one, upon his breast,
God will take care of you. [Refrain]

∽

From a very grateful couple to our loving friends, much love,

    Betty & Norman

WEEK THIRTY-TWO

October 13, 2020

Good morning, dear friends,

My love of hymns began many years ago as a very young choirboy in the Church of England. I find them a wonderful attribute to my enjoyment derived from poetry. I find that it is not just the singing of a hymn, but what is behind the written word. When I was in the flower industry, three of the farms I managed were in Marianna, Florida. On my stay in Marianna, I attended the Presbyterian Church the first Sunday there and listening to the choir, I was struck by the beauty of the choral anthem. I asked if I could join them for the next eight weeks and was to discover a new way to sing an anthem.

FIRST WEEK - The choirmaster (a lady) distributed a new anthem and we were instructed to take it home and read it often throughout the week. And if the words were of a Biblical source, we were to study the Scriptural references.

NEXT WEEK – At choir practice, we took time to read together followed by discussion.

WEEK THREE – We heard the music for the first time and, as the organ played, we just let the words and music mingle.

WEEK FOUR – We were now ready to sing it all together. By now the familiarity with the piece became enjoyable to sing and we were ready for Sunday morning! What a pleasure to know and fully understand the musical message we were delivering to the congregation. Amen.

In these troubling times we are constantly being called on to turn to our Lord for the answer and the answer is prayer my friends. And that is as it should be. And, we do just that this week with the words of a hymn that has been around for five hundred years. Martin Luther penned these words around 1525 from PSALM 46.

∽

A MIGHTY FORTRESS IS OUR GOD

> *A mighty fortress is our God, a bulwark*
> *   never failing;*
> *Our helper He, amid the flood of mortal*
> *   ills prevailing:*
> *For still our ancient foe doth seek to work*
> *   us woe;*
> *His craft and pow'r are great, and, armed*
> *   with cruel hate,*
> *On earth is not his equal.*

Did we in our own strength confide, our
striving would be losing,
Were not the right Man on our side, the
Man of God's own choosing:
Dost ask who that may be? Christ Jesus, it
is He;
Lord Sabaoth, His Name, from age to age
the same,
And He must win the battle.

And though this world, with devils filled,
should threaten to undo us,
We will not fear, for God hath willed His
truth to triumph through us;
The Prince of Darkness grim, we tremble
not for him;
His rage we can endure, for lo, his doom
is sure,
One little word shall fell him.

That word above all earthly pow'rs, no
thanks to them, abideth;
The Spirit and the gifts are ours through
Him Who with us sideth;
Let goods and kindred go, this mortal life
also;

> *The body they may kill: God's truth*
> *abideth still,*
> *His kingdom is forever.*

~

We pray that these powerful strong words will carry you through the days ahead.

In His love,
    Betty & Norman

WEEK THIRTY-THREE

October 20, 2020

*G*ood morning, dear and loving friends,

I trust these words will find you all safe and well.

I had a short moment of anger this past week, which is unusual for me. I was watching the BBC News to see what was happening to our former homeland, when the reader decided to switch to a report on America. He made a dreadful reference to our country when he said, "Americans say that their land is blessed by God – but now it is blessed by COVID-19"!!! I immediately wanted to retaliate, but it would have been a waste of time. He would never understand the folly of his uneducated statement and most likely find it hard to accept the beautiful fact of our life when I told him that despite all, "WE CONTINUE TO BE BLESSED BY GOD."

Then! I found solace, as I so often do, with words from one of my Hymnals. It is such a blessing to turn to a hymn and find the answer to what is bothering you. This time, the answer came with the words written by Alfred Ackley – "He Lives".

Alfred Ackley was born in New York and taught music by his father before going on to study and graduate from the Royal Academy of Music in London. He actually became a great cellist but was ordained a Presbyterian minister in 1914. He spent a few years with the evangelist Billy Sunday and wrote more than 1,500 religious and secular songs.

The delight with this hymn is that before you read to the end of the first line, you find your feet tapping with the melody. Friends, as we go through this special day for our Country, Alfred Ackley could not have written better words for the occasion. Yes, dear friends, HE LIVES. Please take a moment to go listen to this uplifting, joyous hymn!

Now, the hymn I shall share with you this week to

read together is another good hymn proclaiming the powerful truth that He lives! Christian F. Gellert is the author and though for a while he pursued a life in ministry, he had a terrible memory and, unfortunately for him, preaching from notes was simply not tolerated by the Lutheran Church compelling him to eventually settle in the profession of tutoring. He never did lose his love for his first calling and this was one of the hymns he penned:

JESUS LIVES, AND SO SHALL I

(Verse 1)
Jesus lives, and so shall I.
Death! Thy sting is gone forever!
He who deigned for me to die,
Lives, the bands of death to sever.
He shall raise me from the dust:
Jesus is my hope and trust.

(Verse 2)
Jesus lives and reigns supreme;
And, His kingdom still remaining,
I shall also be with Him,

Ever living, ever reigning.
God has promised; be it must:
Jesus is my hope and trust.

(Verse 4)
Jesus lives! I know full well
Naught from Him my heart can sever,
Life nor death nor pow'rs of Hell,
Joy nor grief, henceforth forever.
None of all His saints is lost:
Jesus is my hope and trust.

∼

In Christian love,
    Betty & Norman

WEEK THIRTY-FOUR

October 27, 2020

Good morning, dear friends in His name,

What is '**Love**'? It has so many meanings in all phases of our lives. To my Dad, who grew up in a very difficult and hard family, he spoke of the time he was invited to meet my Mum's family and heard the word 'love' spoken so frequently. In his 'new' loving family, he witnessed the loving attitude that seemed to permeate everyone present. He always claimed that the occasion proved to be a life-changing experience and his love as a husband and father was unparalleled.

When we speak of the 'Love of God', we also read from the BOOK OF JOHN, the love and brotherhood that existed between John and Jesus. From fisherman to Disciple to trusted friend, John expressed his primary purpose for his writing in JOHN 20:32 "But these are written that you may believe that Jesus is the Christ, the Son of God, and that by believing you may have life in His name."

JOHN 15:13 "Greater love has no man than this, than to lay down one's life for his friends."

JOHN 13:34 "A new commandment I give unto you, that ye love one another; as I have loved you, that ye also love one another."

JOHN 3:16-17 "For God so loved the world, that He gave His only Son, that whoever believes in Him should not perish but have eternal life. For God did not send His Son into the world to condemn the world, but in order that the world might be saved through Him."

. . .

We travel to Glasgow, Scotland for this week's hymn. It is the work of George Matheson. He sadly began to lose his sight as a young man, but the strong desire to preach proved to be much stronger than his disability. During his time in University, he became very attached to a young lady and had his mind set on their future together. However, as he was graduating, he told his girlfriend that his sight had begun to fail at an accelerated rate. Sadly, her response was that she did not want to go through life with a blind man! George graduated with honors in 1862,and fulfilled a distinguished life in the ministry. Among his hymns, he produced one of my favorites – "O Love That Will Not Let Me Go".

The music was written by a Yorkshireman, Albert L. Peace, from Huddersfield (just a few miles from where Betty and I lived). At age nine, he was appointed organist at the Holmfirth Parish Church – Holmfirth is one of our favorite small Yorkshire towns.

~

O LOVE THAT WILL NOT LET ME GO

> O love that will not let me go,
> I rest my weary soul In Thee,
> I give Thee back the life I owe,

That in Thine ocean depths its flow,
May richer, fuller be.

O light that followest all my way,
I yield my flickering torch to Thee.
My heart restores it's borrowed ray,
That in Thy sunshine's blaze its day
May brighter, fairer be.

O joy that seeketh me through pain,
I cannot close my heart to Thee
I trace the rainbow through the rain,
and feel the promise is not vain
That morn shall tearless be.

O cross that lifted up my head,
I dare not ask to fly from Thee,
I lay in dust life's glory dead.
And from the ground there blossoms red
Life that shall endless be.

∼

Love and blessings,
    Betty & Norman

WEEK THIRTY-FIVE

November 3, 2020

A good Tuesday morning, dear friends,

This week Betty and I tried something else to ward off the isolation. We chose to watch YouTube on the computer and as a result watched many of the programs that we enjoyed on our visits to the U.K. over the years. One we particularly enjoyed was about a professional gardener. His claim to fame is to find folks who are too ill to tend their garden, or who spend so much time helping others with their life's problems that they have no time for their own gardens. He sends these people on a few days of vacation and then brings in a huge workforce of volunteers to completely transform their garden, large or small, to a real thing of beauty. It is hard to watch without getting a lump in your throat. The look of disbelief and surprise on the recipient's face is equaled by the look of pure pleasure on the gardener's face. Which, led me to a poem I read as a boy by Dorothy Gurney – she was an English poet and Hymn writer. Her father and her husband were Anglican Ministers.

∼

GOD'S GARDEN

The Lord God planted a garden
In the first white days of the world,
And He set there an Angel warden
In a garment of light enfurled.

So near to the Peace of Heaven,
That the hawk might nest with the wren,
For there in the cool of the even
God walked with the first of the men.

And I dream that these garden-closes

With their shade and their sun flecked sod.
And their lilies and bowers of roses
Were laid by the hand of God.

The kiss of the sun for pardon
The song of the birds for mirth
One is nearer God's heart in the garden,
Than anywhere else on earth.

For He broke it for us in a garden
Under the olive trees
Where the Angel of strength was the
   warden
And the soul of the world found ease.

∼

Would you pray with us: Dear Lord, You know all that we are dealing with. Please help us to accept what we cannot change. Help us and turn our worry into prayer. Let these difficult times not take away our joy. Help us to keep our eyes fixed on You. We give You our stress and ask for Your peace. In the name of Jesus we pray. Amen.

    Perhaps it was a reading of the poem "God's Garden" that prompted Charles Miles to produce one of the loveliest hymns with God's Garden in mind. It is interesting to read that Charles first had the ambition to become a pharmacist and he trained at the Philadelphia College of Pharmacy. And he indeed became a fully qualified pharmacist. However, it doesn't end there. Charles wrote his first Gospel song in 1892. It was published by the Hall-Mack Company and he was no longer serving pills! Music became the rest of his life. In Charles' own words: "It is as a writer of gospel songs I am proud to be known, for in that way I may be of the most use to my Master, whom I serve willingly although not as sufficiently as is my desire."

Enjoy the words of Charles Austin Miles as you sing one of the best.

∼

IN THE GARDEN

>   (Verse 1)
>   *I come to the garden alone,*
>   *While the dew is still on the roses*
>   *And the voice I hear falling on my ear,*
>   *The son of God discloses.*
>
>   (Refrain)

*And He walks with me, and He talks
   with me,
And He tells me I am His own.
And the joy we share as we tarry there,
None other has ever known.*

(Verse 2)
*He speaks and the sound of His voice,
Is so sweet the birds hush their singing.
And the melody that He gave to me,
Within my heart is ringing.* [Refrain]

(Verse 3)
*I'd stay in the garden with Him,
Though the night around me be falling;
But He bids me go through the voice
   of woe,
His voice to me is calling.* [Refrain]

∼

Blessings and love to all dear friends,
   Betty & Norman

WEEK THIRTY-SIX

November 10, 2020

Good morning, dear friends,

Surprise, surprise, friends! As I worked this week towards the end of my book, *Life in America*, I noticed that our first meeting at Tara Woods was January 2014. Six wonderful years of Christian friendship that has been enjoyable beyond measure. Forgive me, I said "my book", well I am writing it, but have been so dependent on my special Betty for so much information. Betty has been a keen 'diarist' for most of her life and continues to be. All in all, I have had 74 diaries – since 1946 – to peruse and I happen to be in every one of them!!

Betty and I went to the drive-in church service last Sunday at Holy Trinity and enjoyed it very much, but it does seem strange singing in your car to a congregation of two! Particularly when we enjoy a full church singing together in such a beautiful, fulfilling way to praise our Lord and Master. I also enjoy reading hymns as I would poetry, but hymns are so special. They are written for the sole purpose of praise and worship.

Colossians 3:16 says, "let the word of Christ dwell in you richly in all wisdom; teaching one another Psalms and hymns and spiritual songs, singing with grace in your hearts to the Lord."

In my traveling days as a singer of "A Sermon in Song", I began every service with Psalm 92:1 "It is a good thing to give thanks unto the Lord, and to sing praises unto Thy name, O Most High."

Mathew 26:30 reads, "And when they had sung a hymn, they went out to the Mount of Olives."

Even if you don't know the tune, it is so pleasant to read the prayerful lines of praise - such as "May Jesus Christ be praised" - written by Edward Caswall. He was a Congregational minister in Birmingham, England, dedicated to serving the poor, sick, and children. This hymn is a simple, but such a meaningful prayer.

~

WHEN MORNING GILDS THE SKIES

When morning gilds the skies,
My heart awakening cries.
May Jesus Christ be praised.
Alike at work and prayer,
To Jesus I repair.
May Jesus Christ be praised!

To Thee my God above,
I cry with glowing love,
May Jesus Christ be praised.
The fairest graces spring,
In hearts that ever sing.
May Jesus Christ be praised!

Be this while life is mine,
My canticle, divine,
May Jesus Christ be praised.
May this the eternal song,
Through all the ages long.

May Jesus Christ be praised!

Amen.

∾

Remember friends, "He who sings - prays twice." I honestly do not know who said that, perhaps I read it somewhere, sometime.

Much love to all, in the name of the Father, the Son, and the Holy Spirit,
    Betty & Norman

WEEK THIRTY-SEVEN

November 17, 2020

*G*ood morning, dear friends,

I trust you are all well and getting through your isolation. Although Betty has kept me busy with her 'to do' list, I think that we all have a little more spare time than usual. We spent some time in finishing up the BOOK OF JAMES which left me wondering. What effects does the better understanding of His Word have on the world? And I thought if the world was together in the process, what a great and wonderful world it would be for all.

But what about 'our' world – which is our community, our family, our friends? In other words, 'our' world is where we live, where we spend our days. What effect can we have on 'our' world?

The truth is that as we better understand God's words, we can really have an impact on our community. The way we accept others, particularly with a smile. A friendly gesture to people who are serving us and a repeated use of the important words "Please" and "Thank you." By adopting a courteous attitude to all. Avoiding small talk and judgement of others and, at the same time speak well of them. As we go through trials, we learn to overcome them through prayer and the same prayers defend us from temptation. We have learned to listen and respond and better understand the need for a stronger faith. Even in our small town we have the opportunity to plant seeds of peace and love wherever needed and watch them grow. We have learned that our God will come nearer to our hearts as we surrender to His will. And, that the rewards are ours through our perseverance.

And finally, we learn that living a righteous life, our prayers become powerful and most important – EFFECTIVE!

Working on the BOOK OF JAMES has been an enjoyable study and I think that Brother James would be pleased with our efforts, even in North Fort Myers. Which brings me to a song and we visit the town where I served in the Royal Air Force – a long time ago! Folliott Pierpoint, although a highly educated fellow, was also very wealthy and never had a job as such. However, he was delighted in writing poetry and religious works. In the spring of 1863, he was sitting on a hilltop outside his hometown admiring the country view and the winding river Avon. Inspired by the view and his thoughts on God's creation and his church, he wrote a hymn.

∽

FOR THE BEAUTY OF THE EARTH

>(Verse 1)
>*For the beauty of the earth,*
>*For the glory of the skies*
>*For the love which from our birth,*
>*Over and around us lies.*
>
>(Refrain)
>*Lord of all to Thee we raise,*
>*This our hymn of grateful praise.*

(Verse 2)
For the wonder of each hour,
Of the day and of the night.
Hill and vale and tree and flower,
Sun and moon and stars of light.

(Verse 3)
For the joy of human love,
Brother, sister, parent child.
Friends on earth and friends above,
For all gentle thoughts and mild.

(Verse 4)
For Thy self, best gift divine,
To our race so freely given,
For that great, great love of Thine,
Peace on earth and joy in heaven.

Amen.

∼

In Christian love,
    Betty & Norman

WEEK THIRTY-EIGHT

November 24, 2020

*A*nd a very good morning, brothers and sisters in Christ,

Would you believe it friends, the turkey farmers are having a problem this year. Due to the downsizing of family gatherings, there is a shortage of smaller turkeys! Nevertheless, families will undoubtably find time to celebrate this special day in our calendar, even if the circumstances of this year present a new challenge.

. . .

PSALM 69:30 "I will praise the name of God with a song; I will magnify Him with Thanksgiving."

PSALM 95:1-7 "Oh come, let us sing to the LORD; let us make a joyful noise to the rock of our salvation! Let us come into his presence with thanksgiving; let us make a joyful noise to him with songs of praise! For the LORD is a great God, and a great King above all gods. In his hand are the depths of the earth; the heights of the mountains are his also. The sea is his, for he made it, and his hands formed the dry land. Oh come, let us worship and bow down; let us kneel before the LORD, our Maker! For he is our God, and we are the people of his pasture, and the sheep of his hand."

Some of you may have seen "A Prayer for Putting on a Face Mask" by Rev. Richard Bott, Presbyterian Church of Canada. But if not, I suggest giving it a listen or a read. He speaks on viewing masks as a way to express our love for our neighbors, turning it outward instead of the too-easy inclination to become trapped inward, fixated on the inconvenience. For your amusement, here is a short poem called "Ode to Face Masks" by Talis Jones.

ODE TO FACE MASKS

You itch the backs of my soft ears
You steam up my glasses when I breathe
My lungs have to work that much harder
Sometimes wearing you makes me seethe

But then I think of those around me
The lives I could snuff out with an
    uncovered sneeze
The thought has me scrambling to put you
    properly in place
Let no sickness spread from me, Lord
    please

You're a bit unconformable
You certainly don't always fit
But I suppose it's such a simple task
And if it can save even one life, I'll submit

Which leads me to a song I have sung many times over the years, especially for the Sunday nearest Thanksgiving. It was actually written as a poem by P.J. O'Reilly and his friend Stanley Dickson added the music. You may not be familiar with the tune but the words are special.

∼

THANKS BE TO GOD

> *Thanks be to God for roses rare,*
> *For skies of blue and sunshine fair.*
> *For every gift I raise a Prayer,*
> *Thanks be to God.*
>
> *Thanks be to God for lovely night,*
> *For mystic skies of heavenly light,*
> *For hours of dream and deep delight.*
> *Thanks be to God.*
>
> *Thanks be to God for love divine,*
> *The hopes that round my heart entwine:*
> *For all the joy that now is mine*
> *Thanks be to God.*

My Oxford Dictionary defines the following: '**Thank**' – is an expression of gratitude.

Psalm 100 says we are to make a joyful noise unto the Lord. To serve Him with gladness. Enter into His gates with Thanksgiving. For the Lord is good.

A happy Thanksgiving and love to one and all, in His name,

Betty & Norman

WEEK THIRTY-NINE

December 1, 2020

*G*ood morning, dear friends,

My dictionary says: '**Advent**'…an important arrival…the season before the coming of Christ. It was always the time for us kids to brush up on our carols and begin the door-to-door visit around our village, night after night. We would stand at the door and sing a verse or two of a couple of carols and then close by saying, "*Hole in my stocking, hole in my shoe. Hole in my hat that my hair* *sticks through. If you haven't got a penny, a halfpenny will do. If you haven't got a halfpenny – God Bless you.*" Then we knock on the door and wait to see if they liked our carols, and how many pennies they would part with. For many kids in the village, the money they got from caroling would be all they would get for Christmas.

In 1882, a writer named William Hone noted that Christmas carols would soon be an extinct form of music!!! Well he got that one wrong! In truth, he was fighting a tradition that began long before "Jingle Bells"! In fact he was fighting one of the world's oldest traditions.

The first Christmas carol is said to be "Gloria in excelsis deo". It is said that "Gloria" is the song attributed to the angels when they first saw the Christ child. As a carol it is said to date back to 128 A.D. when the first Bishop of Rome, Telephorus, decreed that "Gloria" must be sung in his church every Christmas Day.

Here is "Gloria" written as a prayer:

"We praise Thee, we bless Thee, we worship Thee. We glorify Thee, we give thanks to Thee, for Thy great glory. O Lord God, heavenly King, God the Father almighty. O Lord, the only begotten Son, Jesus Christ; O Lord God, Lamb of God, Son of the Father, that takest away the sin of the world, have mercy upon us.

Thou that takest away the sin of the world, receive our prayer. Thou that sittest at the right hand of God the Father, have mercy upon us. For Thou only art Holy; Thou only art the Lord. Thou only O Christ, with the Holy Ghost, art most high in the glory of God the Father, Amen."

Would you please sing with me a song which is said to have originated in the Monasteries back in the eighth century.

∼

O COME, O COME, EMMANUEL

> *O come, O come, Emmanuel, and ransom captive Israel.*
> *That mourns in lowly exile here. Until the Son of God appear.*
> *Rejoice, rejoice, Emmanuel, shall come to thee O Israel*
>
> *O come Thou Dayspring, come and cheer our spirits by Thine Advent here,*
> *Disperse the gloomy clouds of night, and deaths dark shadows put to flight.*

> *Rejoice, rejoice, Emmanuel, shall come to thee O Israel.*
>
> *O come, Thou wisdom from on high, and order all things far and nigh.*
> *To us the path of knowledge show, and cause us in our ways to go.*
> *Rejoice, rejoice, Emmanuel, shall come to thee O Israel.*
>
> *O come Desire of nations, bind all peoples in one heart and mind;*
> *Bid envy, strife and quarrels cease, Fill all the world with heaven's peace.*
> *Rejoice, rejoice, Emmanuel, shall come to thee O Israel.*

∼

We are all joined as one in our waiting of His coming. Amen, dear friends.

Blessings,
    Betty & Norman

WEEK FORTY

December 8, 2020

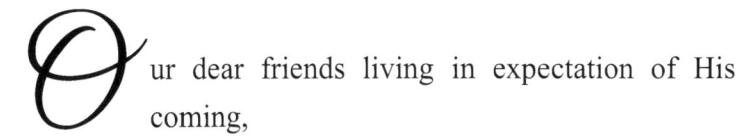

*O*ur dear friends living in expectation of His coming,

I know you don't need a reminder, but this letter (Number 40) is ten months since our last meeting! They say absence makes the heart grow fonder, and I believe that. We have certainly missed our Tuesday mornings together, but the love and friendship we enjoyed so much is not forgotten and we can take comfort in the memories.

I looked for a comment on the Advent season from

my 'old friend' Rev. John Brown regarding the coming of our Savior Jesus Christ. Three hundred years ago he said, "We are so very Blessed to rejoice in a Savior born for us and received into our hearts, and the great salvation which He brings. Also, very happy are the true believers in the pardon of their sins, and the acceptance of their prayers."

We go to a village called Lidget Green for our song this week. The village is about twenty-five miles from where Betty and I originate in the County of Yorkshire. The author, John Fawcett, came from a very poor family but he managed to get a job as an apprenticed tailor when he was just thirteen years old. And he did indeed become a tailor BUT, and there is always a BUT to a good story, at age sixteen he attended an Evangelical meeting. The power and eloquence of the leader's message overwhelmed young Fawcett and there and then he dedicated his life to Christ.

Ten years later, his studies completed, he was to become a Baptist minister. He had a small church in Yorkshire, but had to struggle to support his growing family. Seven years later, he was to receive a call from a much larger church in London. He accepted the call and prepared to move, preached his farewell sermon and had loaded his belongings onto the cart. As the family climbed onto the cart, his wife burst into tears saying,

"John, I do not know how we can leave." John said, "Neither do I." They unloaded the cart and stayed in Yorkshire.

Sitting in his small study a few days later, Dr. Fawcett was moved to write the hymn "Blest Be the Tie that Binds". In these so unusual days, I found peace and rest as I read the very moving lines. Please read or sing with me.

∼

BLEST BE THE TIE THAT BINDS

Blest be the tie that binds
Our hearts in Christian love.
The fellowship of kindred minds,
Is like to that above.

Before our Fathers throne,
We pour our ardent prayers.
Our fears, our hopes, our aims are one.
Our comforts and our cares.

We share our mutual woes,
Our mutual burdens bear.
And often for each other flows,

The sympathetic tear.

*From sorrow, toil and pain, and sin,
We shall be free.
And perfect love and oneness reign,
Through all eternity.*

Amen.

∼

Remember, dear friends, love makes the world go 'round. Love, affection, and kindness to others is what makes life worth living. And they will know we are Christians by our love.

And now for a Christmas Carol!

∼

HAIL, THOU LONG EXPECTED JESUS

*Hail Thou long expected Jesus, Born to set
Thy people free;*

*From our sins and fears release us, Let us
    find our rest in Thee.*
*Israel's strength, Hope of all the saints
    Thou art.*
*Long desired of every nation, Joy of every
    waiting heart.*

*Born Thy people to deliver, Born a child
    and yet a King.*
*Born to reign in us forever, Now Thy
    gracious Kingdom bring.*
*By Thine own eternal spirit Rule in all our
    hearts alone,*
*By Thine all sufficient merit Raise us to
    Thy glorious throne.*

Amen.

∽

God bless you, one and all,
    Betty & Norman

WEEK FORTY-ONE

December 15, 2020

MATTHEW 2:10 "When they saw the star, they rejoiced with exceeding great joy!"

And a very special good morning dear friends.

It is never too early for Christmas carols! In fact, in my childhood, we began our door-to-door singing of carols not long after Bonfire Night (November 5th). Many would tell us to come back at Christmas but there was the whole village to cover, so we pressed on. AND! I am sure that God didn't mind whenever we started singing of the birth of His Son! And we sang "O Little Town Of Bethlehem".

MATTHEW 1:22-23 – The gospel of Mathew, quoting the Prophet Isaiah (ISAIAH 7:14), says, "All this happened to bring about what the Lord had said through the prophet: 'The young woman will be pregnant. She will have a son, and they will name him **Immanuel**, which means '**God is with us**.'"

Perhaps you could join me as we allow our thoughts to trace the path of Phillips Brooks when he travelled to the Holy Land back in 1865. His plan was to be in Bethlehem on Christmas Eve. On Sunday, December 24th, he rode on horseback from Jerusalem heading for Bethlehem. The sun was going down as he approached the village and he stopped for a moment to gaze at his surrounds. It was easy to imagine the shepherds in the fields around him and with the moon and stars shining in the sky, he witnessed a scene just as the shepherds had experienced 2,000 years before. As he paused to take in this very special occasion, he felt a holy hush to his surroundings. He claimed that these few moments never left him for the rest of his life.

The results of his journey stayed with him and he once wrote that, "Again, and again it seemed that I could hear voices telling each other of the 'Wonderful Night' of the Saviors birth." Back in America, the words of a new carol were singing in his mind and came to fruition just before Christmas of 1868 when he wrote one of the loveliest Christmas carols ever – "O Little Town of Bethlehem". As I write, I can almost hear you singing this special carol. Let's sing together friends.

~

O LITTLE TOWN OF BETHLEHEM

(Verse 1)
O little town of Bethlehem, how still we see thee lie.
Above thy deep and dreamless sleep, the silent stars go by.
Yet in thy dark streets shineth, the everlasting Light.
The hopes and fears of all the years, are met in thee tonight.

(Verse 2)
For Christ is born of Mary, and gathered all above.
While mortals sleep, the angels keep, their watch of wondering love.

O morning stars together, proclaim the Holy birth.
And praises sing to God the King. And peace to men on earth.

(Verse 3)

How silently, how silently, the wondrous gift is given.
So God imparts to human hearts. The blessings of His Heaven.
No ear may hear His coming, but in this world of sin,
Where meek souls will receive Him still. The dear Christ enters in.

(Verse 4)

O Holy Child of Bethlehem, descend to us, we pray;
Cast out our sin and enter in. Be born in us today.
We hear the Christmas angels, the great glad tidings tell.
O come to us, abide with us, Our Lord Emmanuel.

I saw this phrase this week and was so reminded of our Tuesday morning gatherings of the past: "We came as strangers and grew together in His name." In His name, Betty and I send our love and Christmas greetings to everyone.

God bless all till we meet again,
    Betty & Norman

WEEK FORTY-TWO

December 22, 2020

Merry Christmas, dear friends, and a good morning to you all,

O the joys of Christmas! But somewhat different this year. From a family of four – Mum, Dad, Daryl, and Debbie – in 1962, we have grown to twenty-three and what a joy when we gather at the Jones' for dinner each year. This year, because of COVID restrictions, we are down to TWO! Nevertheless, Christmas will still be shared via telephone, and computer, and many Christmas presents. AND, there will be a Christmas Eve outdoor service at Holy Trinity Church! So, at four in the afternoon, the cars began to arrive to find a spot in the churchyard and our wonderful family all showed up in their cars. It was to be the first time I had sung "O Holy Night" in the open air!

Once again, we turn to MATHEW 1:18-25 for the story of Christmas:

> Now the birth of Jesus Christ was on this wise: When as his mother Mary was espoused to Joseph, before they came together, she was found with child of the Holy Ghost. Then Joseph her husband, being a just man, and not willing to make her a public example, was minded to put her away privily.
>
> But while he thought on these things, behold, the angel of the Lord appeared unto him in a dream, saying, Joseph, thou son of David, fear not to take unto thee Mary thy wife for that which is conceived in her is of the Holy Ghost. And she shall bring forth a son, and thou shalt call his name JESUS for he shall save his people from their sins.
>
> Now all this was done, that it might be fulfilled which was spoken of the Lord by the prophet, saying, Behold, a virgin shall be with child, and shall bring forth a son, and they shall call his name Emmanuel, which being interpreted is, God with us. Then Joseph being raised from sleep did as the angel of the Lord

had bidden him, and took unto him his wife and knew her not till she had brought forth her firstborn son and he called his name JESUS.

AMEN.

As a child, I always enjoyed the Christmas carol "Good King Wenceslas" and it was also a popular one to sing from door to door in the neighborhood, but I never really understood the story. Apparently, the music was first written as an Easter hymn and Wenceslaus was a Duke not a king. But the fact that it tells the story of a Bohemian Duke going on a journey in terrible weather to give food to the poor peasants on the Feast of Stephen (December 26th), I think it belongs in the Christmas repertoire. We can thank hymn writer John Neale for the words and his music editor, Thomas Helmore, for the arrangement.

∽

GOOD KING WENCESLAS

Good King Wenceslas looked out,
On the Feast of Stephen,
When the snow lay round about,
Deep and crisp and even;

*Brightly shone the moon that night,
Tho' the frost was cruel,
When a poor man came in sight,
Gath'ring winter fuel.*

*"Hither, page, and stand by me,
If thou know'st it, telling,
Yonder peasant, who is he?
Where and what his dwelling?"
"Sire, he lives a good league hence,
Underneath the mountain;
Right against the forest fence,
By Saint Agnes' fountain."*

*"Sire, the night is darker now,
And the wind blows stronger,
Fails my heart, I know not how;
I can go no longer."
"Mark my footsteps, my good page,
Tread now in them boldly.
You shall find the winter's rage
Freeze your blood less coldly."*

*In his master's steps he trod,
Where the snow lay dinted;
Heat was in the very sod,*

Which the saint had printed.
Therefore, Christian men, be sure,
Wealth or rank possessing,
Ye who now will bless the poor,
Shall yourselves find blessing.

∿

Merry Christmas, dear friends,
    Betty & Norman

WEEK FORTY-THREE

December 29, 2020

*G*ood morning, dear friends.

EPHESIANS 1:2 "Grace and peace to you from God our Father and the Lord Jesus Christ."

As a boy, singing Christmas carols from door to door, one of my favorite carols was "We Three Kings". I never knew who the three kings were, but I always had the feeling that the householders seemed to like that carol.

Many years later the same carol was to give me a few sleepless nights!

Now for a little history, friends. Betty and I were invited to attend a brand-new Presbyterian Church in the process of opening in North Fort Myers back in 1963. They had decided to hold a 'Hootenanny' as a friendly gathering for potential new members and that is where we showed up. It appeared that someone told the minister to ask the new Englishman to sing something, which I reluctantly did! The only song I knew all the way through happened to be "Home on the Range" – and I sang it. I was immediately asked to join the small choir – which I did the following Wednesday. And, I must admit, I enjoyed singing with them until, for the Christmas service, the choir was performing an arrangement of "We Three Kings" and I was asked to sing the middle verse as a solo! I had never sung a solo in any church in my life. My days as a junior choir boy never included anything such. Now I was about to sing four lines of a song all on my own!

The next Christmas (1964), I was asked to sing "O Holy Night" at the Christmas Eve service and have been blessed and pleased to sing it every Christmas Eve since (fifty six years this year). Betty and I have enjoyed watching our family grow in our church from our first year with two children, to where our family now occupies the first three rows of pews every Christmas Eve.

Many years later, Tabea Korjus, a dear friend of long ago, attended one of my Sacred Recitals and penned her thoughts to me in this poetic reflection:

> My singing is a prayer, O Lord,
> > A prayer of thanks and praise.
> > In music, Lord, I worship Thee,
> > Thy beauty fills my days.
>
> I give my talents, Lord, to Thee,
> > My mind and heart and voice.
> > For Thou alone art worthy Lord,
> > In Thee do I rejoice.
>
> Accept the worship of my heart,
> > Accept my music too,
> > O bless me Lord, and help me sing,
> > Thy love so full and free.
> > And bless all those who listen, Lord.
> > Help them to worship Thee.

As you read this week's letter, please join me in this grand old carol written by John Hopkins in 1857. The words of this carol are a story in themselves.

A WORD AND A SONG

WE THREE KINGS

(Verse 1)
We three kinds of Orient are,
Bearing gifts we traverse afar.
Field and fountain, moor and mountain.
Following yonder star.

(Chorus)
O star of wonder, star of night.
Star with royal beauty bright.
Westwards leading, still proceeding.
Guide us with thy perfect light.

(Verse 2)
Born a King on Bethlehem's plain,
Gold I bring to crown Him again.
King forever, ceasing never.
Over us all to reign.

(Verse 4)
Frankincense to offer have I.
Incense owns a deity nigh.
Prayer and praising, all men raising.

Worship Him God on high.

(Verse 5)
Myrrh is mine, it's bitter perfume.
Breathes a life of gathering gloom.
Sorrowing, sighing, bleeding, dying.
Sealed in the stone cold tomb.

(Verse 6)
Glorious now behold Him arise;
King and God and sacrifice.
Alleluia, alleluia.
Earth to heaven replies.

Amen.

~

And it all began with the second verse of "We Three Kings".

Blessings to all in the true spirit of Christmas,
    Betty & Norman

WEEK FORTY-FOUR

January 5, 2021

Good morning dear friends in Christ,

Once again, the New Year is upon us. We don't know what the new year will bring, but we do know Him who will walk with us into the new year. And we do so with the confidence that we have His Holy Spirit to lead and guide us daily. Do I hear an Amen?

Many years ago, Reverend John Brown wrote of

PSALM 24: "How great is Christ, who is Lord of all. Surely it is proper that all should serve and praise Him."

∼

PSALM 24

The earth *is* the LORD'S, and the fulness thereof; the world, and they that dwell therein.

For he hath founded it upon the seas, and established it upon the floods.

Who shall ascend into the hill of the LORD? or who shall stand in his holy place?

He that hath clean hands, and a pure heart; who hath not lifted up his soul unto vanity, nor sworn deceitfully.

He shall receive the blessing from the LORD, and righteousness from the God of his salvation.

This *is* the generation of them that seek him, that seek thy face, O Jacob. Selah.

Lift up your heads, O ye gates; and be ye lift up, ye everlasting doors; and the King of glory shall come in.

Who *is* this King of glory? The LORD strong and mighty, the LORD mighty in battle.

Lift up your heads, O ye gates; even lift *them* up,

ye everlasting doors; and the King of glory shall come in.

Who is this King of glory? The LORD of hosts, he *is* the King of glory. Selah.

∼

As I wrote this introduction to the first letter of the New Year, my thoughts turned once again to music, singing, hymns, and prayers. Which is not unusual when we realize that hymns are simply prayers set to music. What a beautiful way to pray whether you sing off key or on key – it makes no difference to Him!

I have chosen a hymn that was written as a poem by a young boy somewhere around the year 1100. That youngster went on to become one of the great leaders in the early church. As a Monk, he pioneered the opening of 343 Monasteries throughout Europe and was titled Saint Bernard of Clairvaux for his labors. In 1849, the poem was translated into English by Edward Caswall – an English vicar, and the result is "Jesus, the Very Thought of Thee".

Let us meditate on the simplicity of the words of this hymn, with deep assurance that we are in Him and He in us. These words enable us to face and bravely greet the new year. Thanks to God! Sing loud and don't worry about the neighbors!

~

JESUS, THE VERY THOUGHT OF THEE

*Jesus the very thought of Thee, with
   sweetness fills the breast.
But sweeter far Thy face to see, and in Thy
   presence rest.*

*No voice can sing, nor heart can frame,
   nor can the mem'ry find,
A sweeter sound than Thy blest name, O
   Savior of mankind.*

*O hope of every contrite heart, O joy of all
   the meek,
To those who fall, how kind Thou art! How
   good to those who seek.*

*All those who find Thee find a bliss, Nor
   tongue nor pen can show;
The love of Jesus, what it is, none but His
   loved ones know.*

> *Jesus our only joy be Thou, as Thou our*
> *   prize will be;*
> *Jesus, be Thou our glory now, and through*
> *   eternity.*

∽

What a privilege it is to carry everything to God in prayer. Love and goodness be yours throughout the New Year.

In His precious name,
    Betty & Norman

WEEK FORTY-FIVE

January 12, 2021

*G*ood morning, dear friends in Christ,

Webster says that '**peace**' is a state of mind characterized by the lack of violent conflict and freedom from fear. But our Bibles go a lot further into the question of peace with so many references to these simple five letters:

P-E-A-C-E.

PSALM 29:11 "The Lord gives strength to His people; The lord blesses His people with peace."

. . .

Hebrews 12:14 "Make every effort to live in peace with everyone and be holy; Without holiness no one will see the Lord."

Psalm 37:11 "But the meek shall inherit the earth and, shall delight themselves in the abundance of peace."

James 3:18 "Peacemakers who sow in peace, reap a harvest of righteousness."

Isaiah 26:12 "Lord, You established peace for us, all that we have accomplished You have done for us."

Let me also add the beautiful words of St. Francis of Assisi for our quiet reading:

> "Lord, make me an instrument of Thy peace. Where there is hatred, let me sow love. Where there is injury, pardon. Where there is doubt, faith. Where there is despair, hope. Where there is darkness, light. And

where there is sadness, joy. O, Divine Master, grant that I may not so much seek to be consoled as to console. To be understood as to understand. To be loved, as to love. For it is in giving that we receive. It is in pardoning that we are pardoned, and it is in dying that we are born to eternal life."

In 1954, the husband-and-wife team of Jill and Sy Miller were asked to write a song for the International Children's Choir. Jill, following a very difficult time in her life, wrote the words expressing the profound joy of God's peace in her life. This hymn you may know is called "Let There Be Peace on Earth".

In the 2015 Christmas season, the song was chosen by Microsoft for a children's choir, but they excluded the verse "With God as our Father, brothers all are we." There was a storm of indignation across the country. So, they produced a second version which did included the verse.

Another lovely hymn that speaks on the power of God's peace in our hearts is "Wonderful Peace" written by W.D. Cornell. Born in 1858, he became an American school teacher by the age of nineteen before later turning to preaching in 1879.

~

WONDERFUL PEACE

Far away in the depths of my spirit tonight
Rolls a melody sweeter than psalm;
In celestial-like strains it unceasingly falls
O'er my soul like an infinite calm.

Peace, peace! Wonderful peace,
Coming down from the Father above,
Sweep over my spirit forever, I pray,
In fathomless billows of love.

Amen.

~

May peace live in our hearts and may we share the peace of Christ with everyone we meet.

Betty & Norman

WEEK FORTY-SIX

January 19, 2021

Good morning, dear friends in His name,

A little history lesson this week, and a somewhat personal one. My twelfth Great, Great Grandfather, Samuel Gorton was born in Manchester, England. His study of the bible led him to be minister of the Church of England. Surprising also, he was a lawyer in the English Courts of Law. This was all the way back in 1640, prior to bringing his family to settle in the Colony of Rhode Island and

Providence Plantations. He proved to be a leader in the area and served as President of the towns of Warwick and Providence. His very strong religious beliefs led him to have problems with the Puritan theology and at one time actually led to his arrest along with seven other men who were placed in chains and taken to Boston for trial. He and one of his followers were released but the other six were publicly hanged. Samuel went on to establish his family among the settlers of Rhode Island.

And for so many years, Betty and I thought we were the first members of our family to settle in the United States! And what does that bring to this week's letter, you may wonder? It brought a wonderful new life filled with the love of our Savior Jesus Christ and all it means to be a Christian. Betty and I are Elders of the Presbyterian Church. Our son was ordained an Elder at the tender age of fifteen for his services to youth at our church. And now, many years later, our family has grown from a Mum and Dad and two children to a family of twenty three, where love abounds day by day.

Let us pray: Dear gracious Heavenly Father, we are so grateful for the Holy Spirit that surrounds our family with such love. With Your love, we have lived and worked and met every obstacle, knowing that You would see us through with more love and encouragement. Our strength as a family has grown with You at the center of our lives where we always trust You will be. With Your support, may we continue to be truly blessed, with Jesus Christ at the very heart of our family. Amen.

It is always so interesting to study the source of a hymn. The writer is invariably moved to put pen to paper after studying the Scriptures or perhaps some happening in his or her life. However, this week we have no such history to lean on. Whoever wrote this grand and, might I add, loved song, is unknown. It also happens to be one of the absolute favorites of so many recording artists and still features in the traditional New Orleans jazz funerals. It is thought that whoever wrote the words may well have been inspired by 2 CORINTHIANS 5:7 "We walk by faith, not by sight." Or perhaps from the JAMES 4:8 "Draw nigh to God, and He will draw nigh to you." Regardless of the source, its words have done the job for which I am sure they were intended, simply to bring us closer to The One who makes all things possible in our lives. Amen.

JUST A CLOSER WALK WITH THEE

(Verse 1)
I am weak but Thou art strong
Jesus, keep me from all wrong

I'll be satisfied as long
As I walk, let me walk close to Thee

(Refrain)
Just a closer walk with Thee
Grant it, Jesus, is my plea
Daily walking close to Thee
Let it be, dear Lord, let it be

(Verse 2)
Thro' this world of toil and snares
If I falter, Lord, who cares?
Who with me my burden shares?
None but Thee, dear Lord, none but Thee

(Verse 3)
When my feeble life is o'er
Time for me will be no more
Guide me gently, safely o'er
To Thy kingdom shore, to Thy shore

∽

We trust that this week sees you walking close to Him,
   Betty & Norman

WEEK FORTY-SEVEN

January 26, 2021

Good morning, dear friends,

The interesting thing about the past year has been an increase in contact with families and friends. However, unfortunately at a distance by the use of telephone, computer, etc. But nevertheless, a contact was made. Even our church maintained an outdoor worship service and at the same time broadcast it via computer. It can be said that finally, the computer worked for us seniors when needed!

Which brings me to a well-known phrase to which many have claimed to be the originators. Simply, "Absence makes the heart grow fonder." It can be seen in various documents dating back as much as five hundred years or so. However, many believe that it was Thomas Haynes Bayly who brought the phrase to life in his poem titled "Isle of Beauty" which appeared in 1844.

~

ISLE OF BEAUTY

> What would not I give to wander,
> Where my old companions dwell?
> Absence makes the heart grow fonder;
> Isle of Beauty, fare thee well!

~

How important is the value of a true and loving friendship. And greater yet is our constant relationship with Jesus Christ and His promise of salvation.

. . .

JOHN 15:9-12 "As the Father hath loved me, so have I loved you: continue ye in my love. If ye keep my commandments, ye shall abide in my love; even as I have kept my Father's commandments, and abide in his love. These things have I spoken unto you, that my joy might remain in you, and that your joy might be full. This is my commandment, that ye love one another, as I have loved you."

1 CORINTHIANS 16:14 "Let all that you do be done in love."

COLOSSIANS 3:14 "And above all these put on love, which binds everything together in perfect harmony."

JOHN 3:16 "For God so loved the world, that he gave his only Son, that whoever believes in him should not perish but have eternal life."

William Ralph Featherstone is the writer of this week's hymn. Born in Montreal, Canada, he became a Christian in the Wesleyan Methodist Church as a boy and it is thought that he wrote this famous hymn between the age of 12 and 16. He sent the poem to his aunt in California who passed it on to a publisher. In 1870, the hymn was seen in a London Hymnal by Adoniram Gordon, an evangelist. He was very impressed by the words, but not the tune. He composed the melody that we know today. On a sad note, William Featherstone died at just 26 years of age.

∽

MY JESUS, I LOVE THEE

> *My Jesus, I love Thee, I know Thou art mine,*
> *For Thee all the follies of sin I resign.*
> *My gracious redeemer, my Savior art Thou.*
> *If ever I loved Thee, my Savior 'tis now.*
>
> *I love Thee because Thou hast first loved me.*
> *And purchased my pardon on Calvary's tree.*
> *I love Thee for wearing the thorns on Thy brow,*

If ever I loved Thee, my Savior 'tis now.

In mansions of glory and endless delight,
I'll ever adore Thee in heaven so bright.
I'll sing with the glittering crown on my
   brow,
If ever I loved Thee, my Savior 'tis now.

Amen.

∼

In His love and harmony,
   Betty & Norman

WEEK FORTY-EIGHT

February 2, 2021

*G*ood morning, dear friends,

In my readings this week, I was drawn to the word '**trust**' and the question entered my mind about who and what do we trust as we go through life. Obviously, my parents, who throughout their days, showed me a high level of trust that was never doubted. Also, my dear wife from the day we first met in church. Then I received word that my oldest pal, Alan, had passed away from the COVID-19 virus. A truly shattering event! We started school together as infants, went through all the grades, played on the school soccer team, and were very busy members of the village Youth Club. As teenagers we played tennis on the same team and were both members of the Royal Air Force (different divisions) for two years. After the Air Force we both married our longtime sweethearts. The four of us took vacations together and played lots of golf. Eighty years of friendship and never a disagreement. And that is how we view our relationship with God – A LIFETIME OF TRUST AND FRIENDSHIP – AND NEVER A DISAGREEMENT.

The BOOK OF PSALMS gives us so many assurances of our need to trust and rely on our friendship with God:

PSALM 37:5 "Commit thy way unto the Lord; trust also in Him; and He shall bring it to pass."

PSALM 40:4 "Blessed is that man that maketh the Lord his trust, and respecteth not the proud, nor such as turn aside to lies."

PSALM 71:1,5 "In Thee, O Lord, do I put my trust; let me never be put to confusion...For Thou art my hope, O Lord GOD: Thou art my trust from my youth."

. . .

Psalm 118:8-9 "It is better to trust in the Lord than to put confidence in man. It is better to trust in the Lord than to put confidence in princes."

Psalm 40:3 "And He hath put a new song in my mouth, even praise unto our God: many shall see it, and fear, and shall trust in the Lord."

Psalm 31:1 "In Thee, O Lord, do I put my trust, let me never be ashamed: deliver me in Thy righteousness."

When we take time to study a hymn, we realize that once again, we have a prayer set to music, which gives us another opportunity to sing out our praises to God. This happens again this week when we sing of His unchangeable friendship, His compassion which covers us day and night. He gives us pardon for our sins and peace in return. He is with us day and night and throughout all the seasons. How fortunate we are to be so blessed.

It had to be these wonderful assurances that led Thomas Chisholm to write this week's hymn. He was born in a log cabin in Kentucky and spent time as a school teacher, a newspaper editor, and an insurance agent before he retired. But his hymn "Great is Thy Faithfulness" will live on forever.

∼

GREAT IS THY FAITHFULNESS

>(Verse 1)
>*Great is Thy faithfulness, O God my*
>   *Father,*
>*There is no shadow of turning with Thee;*
>*Thou changeth not, Thy compassions they*
>   *fail not.*
>*As Thou hast been thou forever wilt be.*
>
>(Refrain)
>*Great is Thy faithfulness!*
>*Great is Thy faithfulness!*
>*Morning by morning new mercies I see;*
>*All I have needed Thy hand hath provided;*
>*Great is Thy faithfulness, Lord unto me!*
>
>(Verse 2)

Summer and winter, and springtime and harvest,
Sun, moon, and stars in their courses above.
Join with all nature in manifold witness
To Thy great faithfulness, mercy and love.

(Verse 3)
Pardon for sin and a peace that endureth,
Thine own dear presence to cheer and to guide;
Strength for today and bright hope for tomorrow,
Blessings all mine with ten thousand beside!

∽

May your day be enriched with His faithfulness.

In His love,
    Betty & Norman

WEEK FORTY-NINE

February 9, 2021

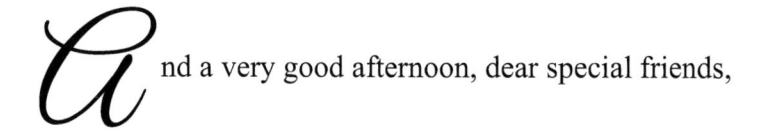

*A*nd a very good afternoon, dear special friends,

Special, because there appears to be a break in our 'confinement' in the very near future. As the vaccine program moves along, there appears to be the possibility of things getting back to normal – if 'normal' is a good word anymore. Nevertheless, we must maintain a positive attitude and, of course, prayer – THE ONE SURE THING – in a changing world.

In these uncertain times we are reminded of ECCLESIASTES 3:1,4-5. "To everything there is a season, and a time to every purpose under the heaven: …A time to weep and a time to laugh; a time to mourn and a time to dance; A time to cast away stones, and a time to gather stones together; a time to embrace and a time to refrain from embracing."

In these uncertain times we are still able to approach the throne of our Savior through our singing according to COLOSSIANS 3:16 "Let the word of Christ dwell in you richly in all wisdom; teaching and admonishing one another in Psalms and hymns and spiritual songs, singing with grace in your hearts to the Lord."

We are so fortunate that through our hymns we can lay our burdens at Christ's feet. The pure joy of singing hymns brings such pleasure as we enjoy praying with music – a special way to tell God what is on our mind. Amen.

The writer of our hymn this week hails from Germany back in the 1600's. Joachim Neander was a young student in the rather rough, unruly days of old Germany. For a prank, Neander and two student friends attended a church service in order to criticize and create amusement. But the words of the minister touched his heart, which proved to be the turning point in his spiritual life. He went on to write many hymns during his lifetime – all in German. We can thank the efforts of a lady called Catherine Winkworth of London for her translations of German hymns such as "Praise to the Lord, the Almighty".

As you sing this wonderful hymn, you can lay your burdens at Christ's feet. Praise the Lord who holds all things in His hands. Let the words dwell in you as you sing.

∽

PRAISE TO THE LORD, THE ALMIGHTY

Praise to the Lord,
The almighty, the King of creation
O my soul praise Him,
For He is thy health and salvation!
All ye who hear,
Now to His temple draw near;
Join me in glad adoration!

Praise to the Lord,
Who o'er all things so wondrously
    reigneth,
Shelters thee under His wings,
Yea, so gently sustaineth!

Hast thou not seen
How thy desires e'er have been,
Granted in what He ordaineth?

Praise to the Lord,
Who doth prosper thy work and defend
    thee;
Surely His goodness and mercy
Here daily attend thee.
Ponder anew
What the Almighty can do,
If with His love He befriend thee.

Praise to the Lord,
O let all that is in me adore Him!
All that has life and breath,
Come now with praises before Him.
Let the Amen
Sound from His people again,
Gladly for aye we adore Him.

Amen.

∼

Just a thought friends, the tune to this hymn seems as fresh as ever to sing and yet this stirring music has been around for a long time. It was written about 1640 in a book by Johann Cruger called *Praxis Pietatis* – Practice for the Glory of God.

Praise to the Lord in His precious name with love,
    Betty & Norman

WEEK FIFTY

February 16, 2021

Good morning, dear friends,

Betty and I were talking this week – we actually talk all the time! We discussed the use of our telephone and the difference it has made to our lives and the lives of so many of our friends during these difficult times. We have experienced a number of days when we have called someone and found them having a 'down day', and the result, the conversation improves the day for them – and us. Thank the Lord.

Sometimes, it is odd where we find inspiration. Such as occasions when we are brought closer to God through an unexpected happening. This week, for us, it was listening to a large male chorus singing most beautifully "I'll Walk with God" from the movie "The Student Prince" of 1954. One rarely expects to find words of such meaning coming out of Hollywood! They were written by a Jewish songwriter, Paul Francis Webster.

The song was labelled as 'popular music', meaning it is expected to appeal to a wider audience. The term 'popular music' was the invention of Tin Pan Alley in New York, aimed at selling as many records as possible. And "I'll Walk with God" did just that. Oddly enough, the singer Mario Lanza, one of the most difficult actors and also an alcoholic (which killed him at 38), sang the song and it sold millions across the world!

So, what did this leave us with? Please take time to prayerfully listen to a recording of this song, read the words, and perhaps even sing along.

Today's hymn was written by James Rowe in 1913. Born in England, he worked in Ireland before sailing for America. A businessman of many trades and talents, he enjoyed penning poems and wrote several thousand before his death in 1933. This may be an unfamiliar hymn to you, but I encourage you to read the words prayerfully and feel the great joy within them.

∼

I WALK WITH THE KING

> *In sorrow I wandered, my spirit oppressed,*
> *But now I am happy – securely I rest;*
> *From morning till evening glad carols I*
> *   sing,*
> *And this is the reason:*
> *I walk with the King.*
>
> (Refrain)
> *I walk with the King, hallelujah!*
> *I walk with the King, praise His name!*
> *No longer I roam, my soul faces home,*
> *I walk and I talk with the King.*
>
> *For years in the fetters of sin I was bound,*
> *The world could not help me – no comfort*
> *   I found;*
> *But now like the birds and the sunbeams of*
> *   Spring,*
> *I'm free and rejoicing –*

I walk with the King.

Amen.

∼

Thought for the day:

Philippians 4: 4-7 "Rejoice in the Lord always: and again I say, rejoice. Let your moderation be known unto all men. The Lord is at hand. Be careful for nothing; but in everything by prayer and supplication with thanksgiving let your requests be made known unto God. And the peace of God, which passeth all understanding, shall keep your hearts and minds through Christ Jesus."

For a second hymn this week, I've chosen one from the pen of Sir John Bowring. He was a Member of Parliament in London and then was appointed Governor of Hong Kong – a very busy life. But he also found time to write many poems and hymns such as:

∼

WATCHMAN TELL US OF THE NIGHT

Watchman tell us of the night,
What it's signs of promise are;

Trav'ler, o'er young mountain's height,
See that glory beaming star!
Watchman does its beauteous ray,
Aught of joy or hope foretell?
Trav'ler, yes; It brings the day,
Promised day of Israel.

Watchman tell us of the night,
For the morning seems to dawn;
Trav'ler, darkness takes its flight,
Doubt and terror are withdrawn:
Watchman, let thy wanderings cease,
Hie thee too thy quiet home:
Trav'ler, lo! The Prince of peace,
Lo the Son of God is come!

Amen.

∼

In the name of Him who shows such love,
    Betty & Norman

WEEK FIFTY-ONE

February 23, 2021

Good morning, dear friends in Christ,

Betty and I had a very lovely start to our morning thanks to Mother Nature and our ever-present Savior. Our garden and the lovely trees, the birds, the rabbits and two loyal Muscovy ducks, and an inquisitive Mocking bird continue to share in our prayers each morning, which prepares us for another day of whatever we find to do that we didn't do last week and the week before that.

The topic of Church Closures and Religion has occupied far more news than usual. And! Isn't it odd that, once again, a spell of adversity can turn most everyone's eyes to our Lord! One lady reporter commented on the subject and called to mind an item that she had read in a book some time ago.

She went on to say that the quotation had proved unforgettable for her. The words were, "GOD GETS US DOWN TO GET OUR ATTENTION AND MAKE US THINK." Those of us that lived through the 39/45 war well remember how the adversity we experienced, somehow, helped fill the churches!

LOCKED IN!! Not a cheerful phrase. But we are blessed with a way out! The walls simply disappear as we pray. What a marvelous gift from God is PRAYER. A gift that has no boundaries. And at a speed faster than any messenger service yet invented, with delivery guaranteed! And the price we have to pay? We paid it when we turned our selves over to His service and promised to follow Him and spread His Word through the way we act and live. Amen.

Psalm 27:1 "The Lord is my light and my salvation; whom shall I fear? The Lord is the strength of my life; of whom shall I be afraid?"

. . .

Psalm 34:4 "I sought the Lord, and He heard me, and delivered me from all my fears."

I am not sure that the great composer Franz Josef Haydn ever thought that his composition for the Austrian National Anthem would ever become the music for our hymn choice this week. As a matter of fact, this tune was the last piece of music the great composer ever played. He was very ill in 1809 and asked to be carried to his piano. He played his famous composition three times and died the next day.

Some thirty years earlier (1779), John Newton chose to write a hymn to Haydn's composition and "Glorious Things of Thee are Spoken" was born. I have always found this hymn to be one of the most singable and expressive in the hymnal. Sing with gusto, friends!

GLORIOUS THINGS OF THEE ARE SPOKEN

Glorious things of Thee are spoken,
Zion city of our God.

He whose word cannot be broken,
Formed thee for His own abode;

On the rock of ages founded,
What can shake Thy sure repose?
With salvation's walls surrounded,
Thou may'st smile at all thy foes.

See the streams of living waters,
Springing from eternal love,
Well supply thy sons and daughters,
And all fear of want remove;

Who can faint while such a river
Ever flows their thirst to assuage?
Grace which, like the Lord, the giver,
Never fails from age to age.

Round each habitation hovering,
See the cloud and fire appear
For a glory and a covering,
Showing that the Lord is near!

Glorious things of Thee are spoken,
Zion, city of our God;
He, whose word cannot be broken,

Formed thee for His own abode.

Amen.

∽

With a song in our hearts for another week, rich blessings to one and all.
    Betty & Norman

WEEK FIFTY-TWO

March 2, 2021

And a very good special afternoon, dear friends,

There appears to be a break in our 'confinement' in the near future! How wonderful it will be to gather again at our Tara Woods clubhouse. It is hard to believe that we have spent the last year – 12 months/52 weeks – in separation due to these uncertain times. Despite the difficulties though, we are still able to approach the throne of our Savior through our singing and praying.

. . .

Psalm 69:30 "I will praise the name of God with a song and will magnify Him with thanksgiving."

Psalm 75:1 "To the chief musician, A Psalm or a song of Asaph. "Unto Thee, O God, do we give thanks: for that Thy name is near Thy wondrous works declare."

Psalm 92:1 "It is a good thing to give thanks unto the Lord, and to sing praises unto Thy name, O Most High."

Perhaps the main reason for including a hymn each week, is the fact that singing hymns in church is one of the activities we have missed most during the past year. It is the singing of hymns that enables us church goers to have, and enjoy, an active part in the service - and our church is a great singing church. And, a joyful way to pray is to sing a hymn! We are so fortunate that through our hymns we can lay our burdens at Christ's feet. Amen.

Our hymn writer this week was a Yorkshireman (Betty and I are Yorkshire born – and proud of it). He hailed from the coastal town of Hull and went to school there to study Civil Engineering, but his love of music caused him to change his plans. He went on to study music at Oxford University and earned his Bachelor's degree. As a dedicated Christian, he wrote around 130 hymn tunes contained in 14 sets of Sunday School Anniversary Hymns. His interest in Foreign Missions led him to write this week's hymn – "We've a Story to Tell to the Nations".

Let us sing now together.

WE'VE A STORY TO TELL TO THE NATIONS

(Verse 1)
We've a story to tell to the nations,
That shall turn their hearts to the right,
A story of truth and mercy,
A story of peace and light,
A story of peace and light.

(Refrain)
For the darkness shall turn to dawning,
And the dawning to noonday bright;
And Christ's great kingdom shall come on earth,
The kingdom of love and light.

(Verse 2)
We've a song to be sung to the nations,
That shall lift their hearts to the Lord,
A song that shall conquer evil
And shatter the spear and sword.
And shatter the spear and sword.

(Verse 3)
We've a message to give to the nations,
That the Lord who reigns up above
Has sent us His Son to save us
And show us that God is love.
And show us that God is love.

(Verse 4)
We've a Savior to show to the nations,
Who the path of sorrow has trod,
That all of the world's great peoples
Might come to the truth of God.
Might come to the truth of God.

∽

Keep a loving song in your hearts, dear friends.
    Betty & Norman

AFTERWORD

Compiling this devotional has been a delightful project that I hope you can enjoy. Reading Scripture, singing hymns, and learning from others – both past and present – is such a fascinating and wonderful way to worship the Lord. To be able to share this book with you brings me great joy – the more one learns about Jesus Christ our Savior, the more one yearns to share about Him! And I only hope it is a little something that can perhaps accompany your own walk in faith.

Speaking of learning from others…many heartfelt thanks to the writers of hymns, poetry, sermons, and other texts referenced throughout this book whom not only contributed to my own learning, reflection, and worship, but will hopefully add to your own growing faith as well.

Though originally these weekly readings were written

in the year of 2020 during the COVID-19 crisis, I feel their messages and encouragements can be appreciated in any time or place (though it does also make for an interesting reminder and insight into those unusual and unexpected times!).

May the Lord bless you and may your love for Christ grow with every day, even during the difficult times you have or may come to face.

REFERENCE LIST

HYMNS
Alphabetized by author.

Ackley, Alfred. "He Lives." Word Music, LLC., 1933, 1961.

Akers, Doris Mae. "Sweet, Sweet Spirit." Manna Music, Inc., 1962, 1990.

Alexander, Cecil Frances. "All Things Bright and Beautiful." Public Domain, 1848.

Anonymous. "Just a Closer Walk with Thee." Public Domain, Unknown.

REFERENCE LIST

Bernard of Clairvaux. Caswall, Edward (Translator). "Jesus, the Very Thought of Thee." Public Domain, 11 A.D.

Blanchard, Richard. "Fill My Cup, Lord." Word Music, LLC., 1959.

Bliss, Philip P. "Man of Sorrows." Public Domain, 1875.

Boberg, Carl Gustav. "O Store Gud." Public Domain, 1885.

Bowring, John. "Watchman, Tell Us of the Night." Public Domain, 1825.

Bridgers., Luther B. "He Keeps Me Singing." Public Domain, 1910.

Brooks, Phillips. "O Little Town of Bethlehem." Public Domain, 1868.

Buck, Carlton C. "I Believe in Miracles." Singspiration Music (ASCAP) (Admin. By Brentwood-Benson Music Publishing, Inc.), 1956.

Carter, Russell Kelso. "Standing on the Promises." Public Domain, 1886.

Caswall, Edward. "When Morning Gilds the Skies." Public Domain, 1854.

Chisholm, Thomas O. "Great is Thy Faithfulness." Public Domain, 1923.

Clark, Frances S. "Enough to Know." Public Domain, 1915.

Cornell, Warren Donald. "Wonderful Peace." Public Domain, 1892.

Crosby, Fannie. "All the Way My Savior Leads Me." Public Domain, 1875.

Crosby, Fanny. "Blessed Assurance." Public Domain, 1873.

Dyke, Henry Van. "Joyful, Joyful, We Adore Thee." Public Domain, 1907.

Fawcett, John. "Blest Be the Ties that Bind." Public Domain, 1782.

REFERENCE LIST

Featherstone, William Ralph. "My Jesus, I Love Thee." Public Domain, 1864.

Gaither, Gloria. Gaither, Bill. "Because He Lives." William J. Gaither, Inc., 1971.

Gellert, Christian Fürchtegott. "Jesus Lives, and So Shall I." Public Domain, 1757.

Giardini, Felice De. "Come Thou Almighty King." Public Domain, 1679 (English 1757).

Handel, George Frederick. "Hallelujah Chorus." Public Domain, 1741.

Hartsough, Lewis (Translator: Ieuan Gwylit/John Roberts). "I Hear Thy Welcome Voice (Gwahoddiad)." Public Domain, 1872.

Havergal, Frances Ridley. "Master, Speak! Thy Servant Heareth." Public Domain, 1867.

Hawks, Annie Sherwood. "I Need Thee Every Hour." Public Domain, 1872.

Hine, Stuart K. "How Great Thou Art." The Stuart Hine Trust, 1949, 1953.

Hoare, Brian R. "Born in Song." Brian Hoare/Jubilate Hymns, 1979.

Hoffman, E.A. "Leaning on the Everlasting Arms." Public Domain, 1887.

Hopkins, John H. "We Three Kings." Public Domain, 1857.

Jackson, Jill. Miller, Sy. "Let There Be Peace on Earth." Jan-Lee Music, 1955, 1983.

Johnson, E. Gustav. "O Mighty God." Public Domain, 1925.

Jones, Ruth Caye. "In Times Like These." New Spring Publishing, Inc., 1944.

Luther, Martin. "A Mighty Fortress is Our God." Public Domain, 1529.

Lyte, Henry Francis. "Abide with Me: Fast Falls the Eventide." Public Domain, 1847.

REFERENCE LIST

Martin, Civilla Durfee. "God Will Take Care of You." Public Domain, 1904.

Matheson, George. "O Love That Will Not Let Me Go." Public Domain, 1882.

Miles, Charles Austin. "In the Garden." Public Domain, 1913.

Monsell, John Samuel Bewley. "Fight the Good Fight." Public Domain, 1863.

Monsell, John Samuel Bewley. "Sing to the Lord a Joyful Song." Public Domain, 1863.

Neale, John Mason. "Good King Wenceslas." Public Domain, 1853.

Neale, J.M. (Translator). "O Come, O Come, Emmanuel." Public Domain, 1851.

Neander, Joachim. Winkworth, Catherine (Translator). "Praise to the Lord, the Almighty." Public Domain, 1680. (Translation, 1863).

Newton, John. "Glorious Things of Thee are Spoken." Public Domain, 1779.

Nichol, H. Ernest. "We've a Story to Tell to the Nations." Public Domain, 1896.

Olds, William B. "He Sent His Word and Healed Them." Public Domain, 1922.

O'Reilly, P.J. "Thanks be to God." Public Domain, 1921.

Palmer, Ray. "My Faith Looks Up to Thee." Public Domain, 1830.

Pierpoint, Folliott Sandford. "For the Beauty of the Earth." Public Domain, 1864.

Robertson, Robert. "Come, Thou Fount of Every Blessing." Public Domain, 1758.

Robinson, Robert. "Mighty God While Angels Bless Thee." Public Domain, 1774.

Rowe, James. "I Walk with the King." Public Domain, 1913.

REFERENCE LIST

Rowe, James. "Love Lifted Me." Public Domain, 1912.

Sammis, John Henry. "Trust and Obey/When We Walk with the Lord." Public Domain, 1887.

Scott, Ann. "Easter." 2020.

Smith, Samuel Francis. "America." Public Domain, 1831.

Smith, Walter Chalmer. "Immortal, Invisible." Public Domain, 1867.

Stead, Louisa M.R. "'Tis So Sweet to Trust in Jesus." Public Domain, 1882.

Walford, William W. "Sweet Hour of Prayer." Public Domain, 1845.

Watts, Isaac. "O God, Our Help in Ages Past." Public Domain, 1719.

Webster, Paul Francis. "I'll Walk with God." Wb Music Corp., 1954.

Wesley, Charles. "Love Divine All Loves Excelling." Public Domain, 1747.

ADDITIONAL TEXTS
Alphabetized by author.

Alexander, Cecil Frances. "Jesus Calls Us O'er the Tumult." Public Domain, 1852.

Bayly, Thomas Haynes. "Isle of Beauty." 1844.

Bonar, Horatius. "I Heard the Voice of Jesus Say." Public Domain, 1846.

Brown, John. "Self-Interpreting Bible." 1778.

Church of England. "The Book of Common Prayer." Public Domain, 1662.

Cranmer, Thomas. "Prayer for the Deliverance from the Plague." 1549.

Cutler, Julian S. "Through the Year." 1854-1930.

God. "Holy Bible" (most referenced translation: New International Version). 1200 B.C. through 1st Century A.D. (NIV, 1978).

REFERENCE LIST

Davies, William Henry. "Leisure." 1911.

Dorney, Elizabeth. "The Chemistry of Character." Pre-1936.

St. Francis of Assisi. "Peace Prayer." 1182-1226. (Possible alternative attribution: Unknown. "La Clochette." 1912.)

Gurney, Dorothy Frances. "God's Garden." 1858-1932.

Jones, Talis. "Ode to Facemasks." 2020.

Jones, Talis. "Why Does God Not Answer?." 2021.

Korjus, Tabea. "My Singing is a Prayer." Unknown.

Neibuhr, Reinhold. "Serenity Prayer." 1932.

"Oxford Dictionary." Oxford University Press, 2010.

Telephorus. "Gloria." 126-137.

Washington, George. 1787.

ABOUT THE AUTHOR

Norman Jones is a proud husband, father, and granddad and he thanks the Lord for the wonderful blessing that is his family – especially his ever supportive wife, Betty, who is his loving partner in all things. Born in Yorkshire, storytelling has been in his bones since he was a lad, as well as a great love for the Lord in his heart, and this book seeks to humbly combine the two passions.

LISTEN & SING ALONG!

Unsure of the melodies to the hymns mentioned in *A Word and a Song* or just looking for music to sing along to? Find a playlist including all of the music referenced in this book online!

You are more than welcome to search for these hymns using any streaming or analog method you prefer, or perhaps you have a hymnal and can play the tunes on a piano or other instrument! If you're unsure where to look however, then we have compiled a playlist to help.

Visit tribloodpublishing.com to find a link for a YouTube playlist including all of the songs in order of appearance in the book for you to enjoy. Discover new musicians, adaptations, hymns, and more as you scroll through and give it a listen. There are even a few songs sung by author Norman Jones!

Printed in Great Britain
by Amazon